Great is your faithfulness

pp 51–52 Sabbath.
a high proportion of this
book consists of quotations
from Matthew Henry & Calvin.

Great is your faithfulness

The book of Lamentations
simply explained

Richard Brooks

 EVANGELICAL PRESS

EVANGELICAL PRESS
Faverdale North Industrial Estate, Darlington, DL3 0PH, England

Evangelical Press USA
P. O. Box 84, Auburn, MA 01501, USA

e-mail: sales@evangelical-press.org

web: www.evangelical-press.org

First published 1989
Second impression 1999

British Library Cataloguing in Publication Data available

ISBN 0 85234-257-8

Typeset by Outset Graphics, Hartlepool.
Printed and bound in Great Britain by Cox & Wyman Ltd., Reading

Contents

Introducing Lamentations

The Old Testament book known as Lamentations is not the most familiar piece of Bible territory for most Christians, although it contains some of the best-known verses in the Bible, such as 1:12 and 3:22-24.

In these opening remarks, therefore, I shall seek to introduce the book to you, before going on to bring out something of its meaning and application section by section. But before we proceed any further it would be of great profit if you would read through the whole book once or twice in order to feel something of its unity, flow and power.

1. The background to Lamentations

In the year 605 B.C. Nebuchadnezzar, King of Babylon, attacked Jerusalem and he spent the next few years seeking to force the whole Mediterranean coastland to acknowledge his supremacy. In this he enjoyed great success.

Then in 597 he made a second attack on Judah, whose eighteen-year-old king Jehoiachin was taken captive to Babylon. Jehoiachin's uncle, Mattaniah, was installed as king in his place by Nebuchadnezzar, who changed the new ruler's name to Zedekiah. Presumably because he was a Babylonian appointee, Zedekiah never really found popular acceptance among the people.

Jeremiah had been called by God to the prophetic office when 'the word of the Lord came to him in the thirteenth year of the reign of Josiah son of Amon king of Judah' (Jeremiah 1:2). That was in 627 B.C., so by the time the Babylonian attacks took place his ministry had become well established. Jeremiah is described by Leon J. Wood as a man of spiritual maturity, courage, deep emotion, compassion and integrity.[1] As an anti-Babylonian party developed in Jerusalem during Zedekiah's reign, urging the king to revolt against Babylon and look to Egypt for help, Jeremiah urged a firm 'no'. But after listening to Jeremiah for a time, Zedekiah finally took his own course and followed the counsel of the pro-Egyptian lobby.

The result was inevitable. Early in 586 Nebuchadnezzar appeared on the scene again and laid siege to Jerusalem. The city fell after a period of eighteen months, in the eleventh year of Zedekiah's reign (Jeremiah 1:3). The fall of Jerusalem is recorded in 2 Chronicles 36:15-20 and Jeremiah 52, along with the fate of Zedekiah and the inhabitants and the exile into Babylon. Both are very important and instructive chapters. We learn, for example, from 2 Chronicles 36 the sort of man Zedekiah was: 'He did evil in the eyes of the Lord his God and did not humble himself before Jeremiah the prophet, who spoke the word of the Lord... He became stiff-necked and hardened his heart and would not turn to the Lord, the God of Israel' (vv. 12-13). And verse 14 of the same chapter sums up the religious state of things in the nation at the time leading up to the exile: 'Furthermore, all the leaders of the priests and the people became more and more unfaithful, following all the detestable practices of the nations and defiling the temple of the Lord, which he had consecrated in Jerusalem.'

That left Judah as a province of Babylon, ruled by Gedaliah, a governor appointed by the Babylonians. But after being governor for only two months Gedaliah was murdered by Ishmael, a member of the royal family. Jeremiah had been given the choice of going with the exiles to Babylon or staying in the land. For the time being he stayed put. After Gedaliah was killed, some of the people became fearful of Babylonian reprisals and asked Jeremiah to seek the Lord's will as to what they should do. God's instruction to them was to stay in the land and not be afraid, and not to flee to Egypt, which it was in their minds to do. But the word of the Lord did not suit them. They accused Jeremiah of speaking falsely and went off to Egypt. Having sought to be a faithful shepherd to the people who had remained behind in Judah, Jeremiah accompanied them to Egypt, not because he wanted to go there, but no doubt so that he might keep God's word before them as best he could, even though they were not keen either to hear it or to obey it. This removal to Egypt, following after the earlier exile to Babylon, left the land of Judah very seriously depopulated.

2. The subject of Lamentations

The great theme running through Jeremiah's prophecy is that of judgement against Judah, which would come in the form of a chastisement from the army from the north, that is, the Babylonians. The people deserved God's punishment because of their idolatry and forsaking of the Lord.

In Jeremiah 25:8-11 we have this key statement: 'Therefore the Lord Almighty says this: "Because you have not listened to my words, I will summon all the peoples of the north and my servant Nebuchadnezzar king of Babylon," declares the Lord, "and I will bring them against this land and its inhabitants and against all the surrounding nations. I will completely destroy them and make them an object of horror and scorn, and an everlasting ruin. I will banish from them the sounds of joy and gladness, the voices of bride and bridegroom, the sound of millstones and the light of the lamp. This whole country will become a desolate wasteland, and these nations will serve the king of Babylon for seventy years."'

In the book of Lamentations, 'The destruction of Jerusalem in the year 586 and the lot of its population are bewailed. It is well to notice that not only the wretched condition of the people is lamented, but also the sin which had brought it about.'[2] Moreover, the book 'represents the attitude of a devout believer in the theocracy towards the destruction of that theocracy. The nation has become so vile that the Lord has left His sanctuary, and evil forces have destroyed it. The poet laments deeply that the nation has become thus iniquitous, but he realizes that the Lord is righteous. He thus calls upon the people to repent. At the same

time he sees how evil has been the action of those who have
destroyed the holy city, and calls for their punishment. This is
one of the most tragic books in the Bible.'[3]

In the Hebrew Bible Lamentations was placed third among
the five *Megilloth,* and was read on the ninth day of the month
Ab, the day of mourning over the destruction of the temple.[4]

3. The author of Lamentations

Scripture does not tell us who the author is, so in effect the
book is anonymous. Perhaps it should stay that way, though
I am fully persuaded that the prophet Jeremiah is himself the
Spirit-inspired penman, and am proceeding with this commentary on that basis. The Septuagint (the Greek translation
of the Old Testament) prefaces Lamentations with the statement: 'And it came to pass after Israel was led into captivity
and Jerusalem was destroyed, that Jeremiah sat weeping and
lamented with this lamentation over Jerusalem, and said ...'

Certainly the author seems to have been an eye-witness of
the city's destruction. There are striking similarities of style
and phraseology between Jeremiah's prophecy and Lamentations, and both books exhibit the same tenderness, sensitivity
and sympathetic temper in their authors. Furthermore, they
very much dovetail together: *the prophecy* shows us the care-
free life of the people of Judah, doing their own thing,
shamelessly indulging in idolatry and taking no notice of
God's warnings to them through His prophet, with the result
that they brought upon themselves the ruin that God
threatened; while *Lamentations* shows the appalling reality
and the detailed consequences of God's visitation upon their
sin in judgement.

4. The style of Lamentations

The book is written as poetry, not prose. It may appear at first
sight to be something of a 'one-note samba' or give the impression that the needle has got stuck in the groove. But that
is not really so at all.

Chapters 1-4 are written as what is called *acrostics*, which means that in Hebrew the verses are alphabetically arranged. So in chapters 1,2 and 4 each of the twenty-two verses begins with successive letters of the Hebrew alphabet (in English successive verses would begin with A,B,C etc.),while in chapter 3, where there are sixty-six verses rather than twenty-two, the verses are arranged in triplets, with each triplet beginning with the same letter, and the alphabet being worked through that way (in English verses would begin AAA,BBB,CCC etc.). Chapter 5 is not an acrostic.

Chapters 1, 2 and 4 are *'dirges'* (elegies or funeral songs) and chapters 3 and 5 are *'plaints'*,that is, songs of personal or collective sorrow where, in parts, Jeremiah identifies himself so closely with the people that he recounts their sufferings as if they were all his own personal sufferings.

5. The purpose of Lamentations

I mentioned above that for a period after the exile Jeremiah remained in Judah with those who were still there in order to pastor them and minister to them. Although the kingdom had fallen and it seemed almost as if the covenant of God had been abolished, Jeremiah did not desert the people but continued to discharge his office.

In fulfilment of this ministry he sought in Lamentations to speak to the people of God's judgements, to exhort them most earnestly and passionately to repentance, to encourage them to fresh hope in their unchanging covenant God and, in Calvin's words, 'to open the door for prayer to God, so that the people in their extremities might venture to flee to God's mercy'.[5]

6. The value of Lamentations

Lamentations should become to us a most precious and contemporary book of Scripture, dealing searchingly as it does with abiding themes like the spiritual glory of the church and the tragedy when this is lost, the exceeding sinfulness of sin, the justice and faithfulness of God, the nature of the covenant and the obligations it places upon the covenant people, the folly of resting on our laurels, and much else besides.

Through this book God speaks very directly to the muddled Christianity (and the muddled evangelicalism) of our own day. 'He who has an ear, let him hear what the Spirit says to the churches' (Revelation 2:7).

May the Spirit of God direct our study of His Word together, to the glory and praise of our God and of His Christ.

Brief summary of Lamentations

Chapter 1

Jerusalem is viewed weeping and bewailing her desolate and forsaken condition. Sin is acknowledged as the cause of all her miseries, the Lord's righteousness is proclaimed and there is a plea that her enemies should be punished.

Chapter 2

The reasons for the Lord's anger with His people are set forth, with a full picture of all that He has done to them. There comes a recognition that only the hand that has wounded them can make them whole again.

Chapter 3

This central, and longest, chapter of the book combines further emphasis on the awfulness of God's displeasure with rich words of consolation drawn from His unchanging character. The people are exhorted to examination and repentance, and there is another appeal for divine vengeance upon His enemies.

Chapter 4

The horrors of the siege are depicted with stark realism, as Zion's former splendour is contrasted with the humiliations brought upon her in the fall of Jerusalem. But there is a note struck in the last verse of the chapter which looks forward to the end of the captivity.

Chapter 5

This is a prayer or appeal to the Lord to remember His people, in the context of a further description of her calamities. The book ends with the longing that God would restore His people to their former glory, their former home and – most important of all – their former relationship with Himself.

1.
The death of Jerusalem

Please read Lamentations 1:1-11

'How'. That is the opening word of the book of Lamentations. But it is not the 'how' of questioning ('How? How so? How can this be?') but the 'how' of surprise and agony ('How! How terrible! How awful a state of affairs!'). As Jeremiah reflected upon the fall of Jerusalem he was absolutely overwhelmed. The destruction of any city has some effect upon you. It is a familiar sight on television news pictures – buildings brought down to the ground or else perched in various half-collapsed precarious positions, roofs caved in, debris everywhere, and no signs of life to be seen. It all looks so poignant, so tragic, so desperate. It is difficult not to be moved, even though, as I say, the sight is so familiar now, that the danger arises of familiarity breeding contempt.

But when it is your own city, the place, maybe, where you were born or converted or married, a place of family background or childhood associations, a place of rich and fond memories, a place that for one reason or another you have in your heart – then it is a very different matter. Things take on a whole new perspective and weight of feeling.

The destruction of any city in Judah would have grieved Jeremiah, but the fact that it was Jerusalem – Zion, the city of God, chosen by Him to dwell in – well, that was, as they say, something else. Right from the start, therefore, the theme of the book is established: the terrible and unthinkable disaster that had overtaken the southern kingdom of Judah and its famous capital Jerusalem. It seemed to be the death of Jerusalem – an event which to many would have seemed as unlikely as that the sun should drop out of the heavens, for, surely, come what may, they thought, Jerusalem was exempt from all danger.

The tragedy is set before our eyes very vividly in these verses, and has as its main features an abandoned city, a deserted sanctuary and a sinful people.

An abandoned city

One stark image is piled upon another in verses 1-3 and the result is tremendously powerful.

The city is *deserted* (1:1). Once it had been bustling with life, full of people, throbbing, vibrant, colourful, as religious, business, commercial and family life flourished. It had not only its resident population, but was the city to which the tribes went up (Psalm 122:4) and was visited by great and small from all the nations. Yet now it has become like a 'ghost town' – a strange, quiet and empty place. **'How deserted lies the city, once so full of people!'** The emphasis of the whole expression is one of solitariness, of being left completely on your own, abandoned on every side. Much later, a Roman coin was struck to commemorate the victory of Titus Vespasian over Jerusalem in A.D. 71, which represented the Emperor Vespasian on one side and, on the reverse, a woman (symbolizing Jerusalem, the daughter of Zion) sitting on the ground under a palm tree in a mournful attitude, surrounded by a heap of arms and shields. The inscription on the coin reads *'Judea capta'* ('Judah taken'). That coin could equally well evoke the scene Jeremiah is recording here.

The city is *bereaved* (1:1). **'How like a widow is she, who once was great among the nations!'** How eloquent bereavement is of sadness, loneliness and despair. Cities have traditionally been described as the mothers of their inhabitants, with the king as the husband and the princes as children. Once the king is gone, the city is widowed and orphaned. Furthermore, the condition of the Eastern widow is a pitiable one: her hair is cut short, she casts aside all her ornaments, eats coarse food, fasts and is considered all but an outcast in her late husband's family. So this image of the widow would have struck an immediate chord in Jewish minds. All Jerusalem's literal husbands and children have gone; all her life has expired. Behind this lies the rich biblical imagery of God as the Husband of His people ('For your Maker is your husband', Isaiah 54:5), but Jerusalem no longer enjoys the presence of her Husband. The sense of the presence of God with them, of God delighting in His people – all the raptures of fellowship with the living God are currently things of the past, though the little word **'like'** (or 'as') 'a widow' implies that Jerusalem has not lost her Husband utterly and for ever, but is only parted from Him for a period. There is in that one word a foreshadowing of reunion.

The city is *subjected* (1:1). One moment she was 'great among the nations'. Time was when Judah was ruler of countries like Moab and Edom. They and others were her vassals. She was either greatly loved or greatly feared. Nations took notice of her. Some gave her presents and some paid taxes to her, especially during the flourishing period of the Jewish kingdom under Kings David and Solomon.[1] But things are different now. The **'queen among the provinces has now become a slave'**. Matthew Henry remarks, 'But now the tables are turned; she has not only lost her friend and sits solitary, but has lost her freedom too and sits tributary; she paid tribute to Egypt first and then to Babylon.'[2]

The city is *emptied of all joy* (1:2), having been deserted and left comfortless, without a friend in the world. 'While others are deriving refreshment of body and mind from their sleep, Jerusalem is wide awake, crying and sobbing with grief, harassed by the prospect of nocturnal terrors, and deprived of all human comfort.'[3] The night-time weeping does not, of course, exclude weeping during the daytime as well. But night is mentioned because (don't we know it?) that is the time when grief and sorrow tend to be felt at their heaviest and drive sleep far away.

Who are **'her lovers'**? The description refers to nations with whom Jerusalem made alliances, 'the human support on which Jerusalem foolishly and presumptuously believed she could rely, especially all those nations whose friendship she had so often preferred, instead of trusting in Jehovah'.[4] As such it would embrace the likes of Egypt, Edom, Moab, Ammon, Phoenicia, Tyre and Sidon. But where are they now? **'Among all her lovers there is none to comfort her. All her friends have betrayed her; they have become her enemies.'**

There is an awful irony built in here. Not only had her former lovers and friends abandoned her, but some had even sided with Babylon in assaulting her. It is the way of the world.[5] Jerusalem was described in Psalm 48:2 as 'the joy of the whole earth', but now her joy has been turned into lamentation and mourning. We are reminded of Jeremiah's own expressive lament: 'Oh, that my head were a spring of water and my eyes a fountain of tears! I would weep day and night for the slain of my people' (Jeremiah 9:1). Verse 2 opens with (literally) 'weeping she weeps'. This verbal form accords with the phrase **'Tears are upon her cheeks.'** This is not past grief that has been got over and which time has healed, but present grief, present bitterness, present agony, present heartache which is continually drawing forth fresh tears which are running down her cheeks. Her whole face is never free from them (cf. Jeremiah 9:18-19). In this verse, Jeremiah's lament over Jerusalem becomes also very much Jerusalem's lament for herself. Yet she can neither comfort herself nor are there any to comfort her. And surely there is here an indirect reference to the loss of *the* Comforter.

Just reflect on something here. How welcome and appropriate it is, whenever we are burdened with grief, to have friends drawing alongside us with whom we can share our sorrows, and who will weep with us and apply the consolations of God's Word to us (meditate upon 2 Corinthians 1:3-4 in this connection). But when we are as Jerusalem became, with no friends supporting us any longer, when no one feels for us and, worst of all, when those we thought were our friends, who once courted us and who gave us the impression that they would stand by us at all times and never let us down, abandon us and do indeed let us down – then our sorrow and sadness become much more grievous and heavy to bear. But take heart, believer; we have one Friend 'who sticks closer than a brother' (Proverbs 18:24). The Lord Jesus Christ is the believer's Friend, and He is 'the same yesterday and today and for ever' (Hebrews 13:8).

> But Oh, my friend!
>   My friend indeed,
>   Who at my need
> His life did spend!
>
>   (Samuel Crossman).[6]

Rejoice in this friendship. Do not grieve Him, and remember that 'Anyone who chooses to be a friend of the world becomes an enemy of God' (James 4:4).

The city is *exiled* (1:3) in the land of her enemies who neither know God nor care anything about him. The nation that once was separated from the heathen now dwells among them. The sombreness of **'Judah has gone into exile'** can be felt. Judah stands here, of course, for the population not merely of the city of Jerusalem but of the whole kingdom. God's people are a special people, a distinctive people, a holy people; but now they are mingled among those who worship idols, those who are 'excluded from citizenship in Israel and foreigners to the covenants of the promise, without hope and without God in the world' (Ephesians 2:12).

It seems that the impossible has happened. And, not surprisingly, **'she finds no resting place'** – no joys, no consolations, no sense of being at home, no blessed assurance of the favours of God. All is exactly as Moses predicted: 'Then the Lord will scatter you among all nations, from one end of the earth to the other. There you will worship other gods – gods of wood and stone, which neither you nor your fathers have known. Among those nations you will find no repose, no resting place for the sole of your feet. There the Lord will give you an anxious mind, eyes weary with longing, and a despairing heart. You will live in constant suspense, filled with dread both night and day, never sure of your life' (Deuteronomy 28:64-66).

The word for **'distress'**, at the end of verse 3, has the sense of 'straits'or 'extremities' – narrow places from which escape is impossible, or circumstances of life from which no escape can be found. (Compare David's testimony in Psalm 116:3.) What a contrast, too, between the lovers and friends of verse 2 and the pursuers of verse 3. Judah and Jerusalem had become a sitting duck, a target for all her enemies.

A deserted sanctuary

In verses 4-6 the picture gets worse, not better. From the earlier viewpoint of her political and international state, the focus now turns to Judah and Jerusalem's spiritual and

ecclesiastical condition, the poverty of the latter being ultimately of far greater importance than the former.

Look first at verse 4. For a start, **'The roads to Zion mourn.'**
The Authorized Version has 'the ways *of* Zion', but 'the ways/
roads *to* Zion' gives the clearer sense. What is in mind is not
the streets of Jerusalem herself but the roads or highways
leading up to Jerusalem from outside. The city of Jerusalem
was situated on Mount Zion, and whether you approached it
from the north, south, east or west you always went *up* to
Jerusalem. These roads used to be thronged with happy and
expectant worshippers singing the praises of God: 'That is
where the tribes go up, the tribes of the Lord, to praise the
name of the Lord according to the statute given to Israel'
(Psalm 122:4). Whether at the daily sacrifices or at the seasons of the great festivals each year, they were busy with the
pilgrims lifting up their voices in the songs of ascents (Psalms
120-134). But now these same roads are empty, **'for no one
comes to her appointed feasts'**. All is silent and still. Not a
footstep or voice can be heard. Everything about these roads
has become dismal and sad and looks unkept and overgrown.
Latterly those feasts had been neglected and profaned anyway, so that God had spoken some hard words about them
(Isaiah 1:11-17).

This melancholy picture continues in the second part of the
verse: **'All her gateways are desolate.'** Do you remember how
God speaks of His love for 'the gates of Zion'? (Psalm 87:2).
That refers to the gathering together of the people of God to
worship Him and give Him the glory, and the meeting of God
with His people. But no more. As for the literal gateways to
the city, there is nothing doing there either. The merchants no
longer sell there. The people no longer gather there. The
elders no longer dispense justice there. The **'priests groan'**.
There is nothing for them to do any more, for the sanctuary
has been abandoned; the services, ceremonies and sacrifices
have ceased; everything has closed down. And **'her maidens
grieve'**, for their music, singing and dancing are no longer
required either, and gone are their prospective husbands.
The whole place **'is in bitter anguish'**.

Pause again for serious reflection. What a sad sight is a dis-
pirited ministry, pictured here in the groaning priests! Do you
ensure that your own minister's 'work will be a joy, not a

burden, for that would be of no advantage to you'? (Hebrews 13:17). Are you an encourager of the ministry? I do not mean primarily by speaking encouraging words (though there is a place for that, if the glory of God is the aim), but in coming to worship with a prepared and expectant heart, sitting under the ministry, with an open Bible, in a devoted and concentrating spirit, and being not only a hearer of the Word but a doer of it as well. Do you pray for your minister? Do you bless God for him? Do you acknowledge that in the sovereign providence of God, despite all the man's failings and imperfections (which perhaps in many cases are remarkably like your own), he has been set apart for the work and you have not? (This is, dare I say it, a very necessary acknowledgement in these days when evangelicalism is invaded with the spirit that insists that almost anyone in the membership of the congregation can do the minister's work better than the minister himself.) Do you support him generously as he seeks to give himself wholeheartedly and self-denyingly to the work of God, including the care of your eternal soul?

In proportion to the misfortune and humiliation of Judah is the success and prosperity of her enemies (1:5). **'Her foes have become her masters; her enemies are at ease'**, as was threatened if God's people were unfaithful to Him. 'The Lord will make you the head, not the tail. If you pay attention to the commands of the Lord your God that I give you this day and carefully follow them, you will always be at the top, never at the bottom' (Deuteronomy 28:13); but otherwise the opposite applies and their enemy 'will be the head, but you will be the tail' (Deuteronomy 28:44). So, as if the sorrows of God's people were not dark enough, things are made worse by the brilliant prosperity of their enemies. But 'This advantage on the part of her enemies had not happened by chance, nor by mere arbitrariness or unrighteousness on the side of God, but by an act of Divine rectitude in the punishment of Israel for their sins.'[7] **'The Lord has brought her grief because of her many sins.'** We shall see this in more detail from verse 8 onwards. The awful effect of exile is seen too in the splitting up of families, which is hinted at in the final part of the verse – children torn away from parents, families cast asunder. **'Her children have gone into exile, captive before the foe.'**

But what is the worst thing to have happened? What has

[handwritten margin note: The voice of an unhappy pastor?]

Zion lost which indicates just how bad things have become? Verse 6 tells all: Zion has lost her glory. **'All the splendour has departed from the Daughter of Zion.'** She who is, by her very nature, 'all glorious ... within' (Psalm 45:13); she who is 'a crown of splendour in the Lord's hand, a royal diadem in the hand of your God' (Isaiah 62:3); she whose name is Hephzibah (which speaks of God's delight in her) and Beulah, telling of God's marriage covenant with her (Isaiah 62:4) – *this Zion* has now lost all her beauty and glory. God had chosen her as a habitation for Himself. The psalmist records of Him that He 'is in her citadels; he has shown himself to be her fortress'; she is 'the city of the Lord Almighty ... the city of our God: God makes her secure for ever' (Psalm 48:3,8). Surely it is this very presence of God Himself among His people and, not least, His manifesting of Himself in His felt presence and power as His people come before Him to worship Him 'in the splendour of his holiness' (Psalm 29:2) that constitutes, above all, the splendour of Zion. And so it would be true to say, in the present context, that the splendour departed from the Daughter of Zion when God forsook His people, allowed the temple to be destroyed and discontinued the ordinances of worship.

This is all underscored in the reference to **'her princes'**, which I take to refer to Zedekiah, King of Judah, and all his soldiers, who fled from Jerusalem but were recaptured within a few miles of the city, having failed to make good their escape (Jeremiah 39:1-7, 2 Kings 25:1-7). These men, who had been regarded as a vital part and parcel of the strength of Jerusalem, **'are like deer that find no pasture; in weakness they have fled before the pursuer'**. Reading that, you cannot help thinking, by way of contrast, of that matchless picture in the 23rd Psalm of the Lord Jesus Christ. How quickly a startled and frightened deer takes to flight, but He is the unfailing and unchangeable Shepherd of His people, leading and directing them, making every provision for them and never failing or forsaking them. How thankful we are for Him!

But why this alarming change? What could the covenant people of God have done to be in this appalling condition and position? That brings us to our next section.

A sinful people

Coming to verses 7-11, we are reminded of Proverbs 14:34: 'Righteousness exalts a nation, but sin is a disgrace to any people.' It has already been stated in verse 5 concerning Zion that 'The Lord has brought her grief because of her many sins,' and that says it all. It always does and it always will. The sequence is always so plain: the Lord our God is holy; His people have turned against Him; so He must punish sin. In a phrase, *the people are God-forsaken because they have become God-forsaking.* That principle always abides and applies. It is an invariable rule. Look at the way the people's sin is described: she has **'sinned greatly'** (literally, 'sinned a sin') **'and so has become unclean'** (v.8); mention is made of **'her nakedness'**, for all to see (v.8), and **'her filthiness'** and **'her fall'** (v. 9). What does all this mean? Let us look at it verse by verse.

Jerusalem has become *an object of derision* (1:7). There is a heart-rending contrast here. **'In the days of her affliction and wandering'** draws from Laetsch the remark: 'They had loved to roam (Jeremiah 2:31) – now they are condemned to roam.'[8] Jerusalem looks back and **'remembers all the treasures that were hers in days of old'** (the times of Moses and Joshua, David and Solomon), but now 'in the days of her affliction and wandering', or 'unrest', the situation is very different. She is in enemy hands. No one comes to her aid. **'There was no one to help her.'** And her enemies merely **'looked at her and laughed at her destruction'**.[9] How the world loves to gloat over the calamities of God's people!

Jerusalem could not help remembering the **'days of old'**, with their treasures and blessings – the days of former prosperity. But, of course, that very remembrance brought comfort and increase of sorrow both together. There is an important spiritual principle here. How tragic it is that we so often only value the precious things of God when we have lost the felt sense of them or had the full enjoyment of them taken away for a season! Sorrow's crown of sorrow is remembering happier days, someone has said.

Only now, in their days of extremity, did God's people consider the mercies of God that they had formerly possessed.

God often awakens such reflection by means of affliction, in
order to draw us afresh to Himself, and this in itself is a token
of His mercy, even though enjoyed in the midst of tears.

> Where is the blessedness I knew
> When first I saw the Lord?
> Where is the soul-refreshing view
> Of Jesus and His Word?

(William Cowper).

Jerusalem has been *stripped naked of her glory* (1:8). And
she brought it all upon herself! Harrison urges that the
'nakedness' here has the sense of 'ill repute' and remarks that
'The proud female has become a fallen woman through par-
ticipating in the demoralizing rites of Baal worship.' We could
describe that nakedness as her sins and vices that have now
come to the light, in the obvious sense that nakedness speaks
of everything being laid bare and secret and covered things
being revealed. The higher you stand, the further you fall.
When the glory of the church (God's own glory displayed in
her) is defiled by sin, then how grievous is the fall, how shock-
ing is the contrast, how appalling is the defilement!

And, what only adds to the awful irony, when the church
sins and becomes like the world, the world does not honour
her, applaud her or congratulate her – not usually, anyway.
Instead, the world despises her and **'she herself groans and
turns away'** in shame. Her honour is in her separateness, her
holiness, her distinctiveness, and the world, in its strange
way, knows this and recognizes this. But the church becoming
like the world or, worse still, the church playing at being the
world, is one of the most pathetic sights under the sun.

Jerusalem has been *spoiled by her enemies* (1:9-10). It is not
that the people of God, bound to Him in everlasting covenant, were unaware of their obligations of obedience and holiness, or of the penalty for failure to attend to such obligations.
Again and again God had warned them and instructed them
through His prophets. Yet **'Her filthiness clung to her skirts;
she did not consider her future.'** The mention of the skirts
speaks again of her sin now being out in the open for all to see.
With the second part of the statement, compare
Deuteronomy 32:29: 'If only they were wise and would

understand this and discern what their end will be!' The result is that **'her fall was astounding'** (AV, 'she came down wonderfully'). The word 'astounding', or 'wonderfully', impresses upon us the awesomeness of it all. She was cast down in an extraordinary manner. Can this really have happened? Yes, indeed! As a consequence of all this, an earnest cry is put into the mouth of Jerusalem herself at the end of verse 9: **'Look, O Lord, on my affliction, for the enemy has triumphed.'**

The punishment and humiliation of Jerusalem received a further focus in the spoiling of **'her treasures'** (the word means 'valuables') and – horror of horrors! – the invading and plundering of **'her sanctuary'**. The 'treasures' would be the vessels and treasures of the temple (Jeremiah 52:17-23; Isaiah 64:11; 2 Chronicles 36:10). The 'sanctuary' refers to the sacred precincts of the temple that no pagans or foreigners were ever to enter. For that matter even Israelites themselves who did not belong to the priesthood were forbidden to enter the sanctuary, so what a pollution it was for invading Babylonian armies to march in! They had no right to be there even for worship, let alone for purposes of destruction!

And, finally, Jerusalem was *left without even the bare necessities of life* (1:11). **'Treasures'** here is the same word we have just had in verse 10 (a rare Hebrew word, only ever found in the plural), though the reference this time is to the people selling their own personal, prized and valuable possessions. For what purpose? For the most basic one of buying necessary **'food to keep themselves alive'** (AV, 'to relieve [refresh, recover] the soul'). With the inhabitants having been starved into a surrender, famine conditions were now obtaining, and food became the most desired and needed commodity of all. Anything and everything had to go, if it was either that or no food. Back in verse 4 we found the priests groaning. Then in verse 8 Jerusalem herself was represented, poetically, as groaning. Now, in verse 11, **'all her people groan'** in their desperate extremity. We can hear echoes of Job 2:4: 'A man will give all he has for his own life.'

Once again the people cast themselves upon the Lord: 'Look, O Lord, and consider, for I am despised.'

How awful sin is! We should be in no doubt about that – not least from the picture here of God's punishment of it. But there is a difference between unbelievers and believers being punished for their sins. The unbeliever in one sense 'mourns' his punishment, as a consequence of his sin, but becomes bitter and hardened, reckons himself to be hard done by and eventually charges God with being unfair. But the believer should not become hardened but rather be caused to consider his ways and to examine his life. He makes good use of Psalm 139:23-24, prostrates himself, humbles himself beneath God's mighty hand, acknowledges the justice of God's punishment and crying, 'God, have mercy on me, a sinner' (Luke 18:13), seeks God's face with that godly sorrow that brings repentance (2 Corinthians 7:10).

Looking at verses 8-11, we cannot but ask: if this is the account God takes of sin in His own people, what will be the end of those who refuse to obey the gospel of God? (2 Thessalonians 1:8-10). Sin does pay its wages. Boomerangs do come back!

Notice how verses 9 and 11 both represent Jerusalem calling upon the Lord in her sin and her need. What a mercy it is when the eyes of a sinner are opened to see his sins as the cause of his trouble, and he cries to God for help! With what gracious speed does the Lord God come to the sinner's aid, and when the sinners are found among His own people, how fully and freely He heals their backslidings! 'The only way to make ourselves easy under our burdens,' remarks Matthew Henry, 'is to cast them upon God first, and leave it to him to do with us as seemeth good.'

The metrical version of the opening of Psalm 40 puts it this way:

> I waited for the Lord my God
>   And patiently did bear;
> At length to me He did incline
>   My voice and cry to hear,

and continues to this climax:

> O Lord my God, full many are
>   The wonders Thou hast done;
> Thy gracious thoughts to usward far
>   Above all thoughts are gone.

Thy tender mercies, Lord, from me
Oh, do Thou not restrain;
Thy loving-kindness and Thy truth,
Let them me still maintain.

Before we leave this first section of Lamentations, let me make one further comment regarding the whole passage, for there is an application which we must make, since this is no dead historical set-piece. Is not so much of the contemporary church reflected here – her waywardness in abandoning God's absolute laws; her worldliness, as she allows herself to be taken over by carnality and gimmicks and is both proud and at the same time a pathetic spectacle; and her crazy ecumenical policies aimed at destroying the distinctiveness of the true church of God, in terms both of doctrinal purity and holy living? Has she not become a laughing-stock, so often regarded as impotent, with nothing to say and nothing firmly believed any longer? Again, she is God-forsaken because God-forsaking. Times do not change, and nor does God.

In this connection, and with the phrase 'The roads to Zion mourn' (1:4) very much in mind, there are few more depressing spectacles than to see closed-down churches and chapels either with weeds and grasses growing around the entrance, or else sold off as carpet warehouses, cinemas, mosques and for all manner of other uses. It is even more dismal and poignant when you have seen or can remember in the past that same sanctuary filled with delighted worshippers, God enthroned upon His people's praises. Truly when men forsake the house of God, God forsakes it too, and then it is utterly forsaken. 'Ichabod' ('no glory', 'the glory has departed', 1 Samuel 4:21-22) is written all over it.

There is a solemn *warning* for us in all this. Since the Lord could, and did, destroy Jerusalem without being unfaithful to His promises to her forefathers about the security of His dwelling-place, just so He can, and does, remove the lampstands from the churches (Revelation 2:5), denominations and congregations, without breaking His glorious promise given to the true church as a whole that the gates of hell shall not prevail against it (Matthew 16:18).

We also have here an urgent *call to prayer*. How we need to look to the Lord over the deformity of His church, crying to Him for mercy, pleading with Him to restore His beauty to Zion (that is, to us, His people), relying upon His promises and believing that our prayers are not in vain! Let Isaiah 62:1 and Habakkuk 3:2 start us off!

O Breath of life, come sweeping through us,
    Revive Thy church with life and power.
O Breath of life, come, cleanse, renew us,
    And fit Thy church to meet this hour.

O Wind of God, come, bend us, break us,
    Till humbly we confess our need;
Then in Thy tenderness remake us,
    Revive, restore; for this we plead.

O Breath of Love, come breathe within us,
    Renewing thought and will and heart;
Come, love of Christ, afresh to win us,
    Revive Thy church in every part.

Revive us, Lord! Is zeal abating
    While harvest fields are vast and white?
Revive us, Lord! The world is waiting,
    Equip Thy church to spread the light.

                          (Bessie P. Head).

2.
'The Lord is righteous'

Please read Lamentations 1:12-22

The theme of the nation's desperate condition continues as we move into the second half of the first chapter, though with what we might call a change of direction. The first section ended in verse 11 with the poignant lament: 'Look, O Lord, and consider, for I am despised,' as Jerusalem's cry went up to God. The second section begins in verse 12 with the equally poignant plea: 'Is it nothing to you, all you who pass by?', as Jerusalem now cries out to the people round about her. Two acknowledgements are made now more dogmatically than has been expressed so far: what the Lord has done, and what His people have done.

What the Lord has done

Notice, to start with, the number of times in which the Lord's name appears in verses 12-18 – count them up for yourself – along with the occurrences of the personal pronoun 'He' and the possessive 'His' referring to the Lord. Although we have had the statement already in verse 5, 'The Lord has brought her grief because of her many sins,' this whole theme is now opened up far more fully and frankly. It is very much a case of 'The Lord has done this' (Psalm 118:23).

Exactly what is it that the Lord has done?

The Lord has inflicted remarkable suffering upon His people

He has done this **'in the day of his fierce anger'**, or the day of His indignation, or great heat. Only this explains the unparalleled nature of Israel's sorrow and suffering, which this verse

12 draws out so plaintively: '**Look around and see. Is any suffering like my suffering that was inflicted on me, that the Lord brought on me in the day of his fierce anger?**'

The fierce anger of the Lord is a terrifying reality. His wrath is His holiness stirred into activity against sin. Do not miss the fundamental connection between God's wrath and His holiness. It is precisely because He is a holy God that He is a God of fierce anger, for He cannot have anything to do with sin in His presence. So the prophet here, in the name of God's lamenting people, looks beyond the sufferings and afflictions themselves and, in Matthew Henry's words, 'owns them all to be directed, determined and disposed of by God'.

But there is a further word that needs to be added on this verse. The words with which the verse opens, 'Is it nothing to you, all you who pass by?', have been very freely and popularly applied, in preaching, hymnody and much evangelical thinking generally, to the sufferings of the Lord Jesus Christ. What are we to say to this? Ultimately, that it is not to be commended. This may seem a harsh judgement, for two reasons. One is that these words bring Christ's own lament over Jerusalem very much to mind. We have it in Matthew 23:37-38: 'O Jerusalem, Jerusalem, you who kill the prophets and stone those sent to you, how often I have longed to gather your children together, as a hen gathers her chicks under her wings, but you were not willing. Look, your house is left to you desolate.' The other reason, perhaps more significant, is that there never has been and never will be any suffering like Christ's suffering. His sufferings were indeed absolutely without parallel – the sinless One dying for the guilty to bring us to God, God's own Son Himself bearing our sins in His body on the tree, God making Him who had no sin to be sin for us. Calvary is unique. Christ's sufferings are unique. He died as our Saviour, our substitute, our sin-bearer.

> We may not know, we cannot tell,
> What pains He had to bear;
> But we believe it was for us
> He hung and suffered there.
>
> (Cecil F. Alexander).

I remember several years ago now being asked by a Christian doctor in the city in which I was ministering at the time to go and counsel a woman who was in a bad way for a whole variety of reasons, but whose problems, in the judgement of the doctor, were primarily spiritual ones caused by sin. In speaking to her of the work of Christ, of His sufferings and sacrifice, and of her own urgent need of Christ, I was fairly shattered to hear her insist that He had not had to go through anything like the suffering that she was familiar with!

I urge again that the sufferings of Christ were unparalleled and unspeakable. There is no doubting that truth. It is as solemn as it is glorious, as awesome as it is magnificent. And it would seem at first glance (and certainly at a sentimental glance) to fit verse 12. But think carefully, and do not let wishful thinking in your heart carry you away in this instance. Remember that the original context of the book of Lamentations has nothing to do with the sufferings of Christ for His people. Remember, too, that when He did suffer, the Lord Jesus Christ made no attempt whatsoever to draw attention to Himself as peculiarly afflicted, whereas that is precisely the spirit of this verse. Christ's call was, 'Daughters of Jerusalem, do not weep for me; weep for yourselves and for your children' (Luke 23:28). I have to agree with an old writer who remarks that the application of this verse in any direct way to Christ is 'merely an accommodation of the words'.

The Lord has caused His people to feel His displeasure

Two vivid images are used in verse 13 – fire and a net. First of all, **'From on high he sent fire, sent it down into my bones,'** causing her pain and making her waste away as with a fever. The 'from on high' underscores the divine origin and nature of the punishment – heavenly fire burns more fiercely than earthly and cannot be quenched so easily. The image of fire is suggested naturally by the last words of the preceding verse, where **'fierce anger'** could also be translated 'glowing' or 'burning anger'. And the bones stand for penetration into the innermost parts. David cried, 'Be merciful to me, Lord, for I am faint; O Lord, heal me, for my bones are in agony' (Psalm 6:2), while Hezekiah testified, 'I waited patiently till dawn, but like a lion he broke all my bones' (Isaiah 38:13). God was not dealing with the people in some light or superficial way.

He meant business, if I may put it that way. His dealings were being felt, in the deepest sense.

The second image comes from the world of the hunter, who sets out to trap the animals or beasts he is after by spreading a net for them. Similarly, the Lord **'spread a net for my feet and turned me back'**, with the result that the more Jerusalem tried to extricate herself from her predicament by her own efforts, by the application of her own wisdom, her self-justification, and so on, the more entangled she became and the worse matters were. Is that not always the case?

And the effect of this? **'He made me desolate, faint all the day long'**, evoking the pictures of friendlessness, loneliness, isolation and lack of strength which have already been described in this first chapter.

The Lord has turned the sins of His people into a yoke

The metaphor this time is taken from agricultural life (1:14). The opening statement of the verse is difficult to translate. Some manuscripts modify the Hebrew consonants of the verb, leading to the translation: 'Watch has been kept over my transgressions' (cf. NIV footnote). Another reading of the verb would bring the translation: 'He has made heavy the yoke of my transgressions.' But the NIV captures it well with **'My sins have been bound into a yoke; by his hands they were woven together.'** Again the emphasis is upon the Lord's doing. We may observe in passing that it is the general name of God, *Adonai,* and not the covenant name, Jehovah, which the people utter here. This title occurs fourteen times by itself in Lamentations, while the two names appear together in Jeremiah's prophecy. Why? We do not know. The suggestion has been made that it is because the people in their punishment felt the Lordship of God more and the covenant love of God less. But Lamentations itself does not really give grounds for such a view.

Calvin expresses it like this: 'We ought then to bear in mind the two clauses – that God's hand held the yoke tied, and also that the yoke was bound around the neck of Jerusalem. As when a husbandman [farmer, ploughman], after having tied a yoke to oxen, holds a rein and folds it round his hand, so that the oxen not only cannot throw off the yoke, but also must

obey the hand which holds the reins, so also it is said that the
yoke of iniquities was fastened.' The ox could get furious,
kick and struggle, but it could not loose itself from the yoke.
So it is in the spiritual life. God binds our sins into a yoke,
fastens that yoke upon us and holds it by His own hands, as it
were, so that we cannot escape from it.

Matthew Henry is another one who is helpful in drawing
this picture out: 'The yoke of Christ's commands is an easy
yoke (Matthew 11:30), but that yoke of our own transgressions is a heavy one. God is said to bind this yoke when
He charges guilt upon us and brings us into those inward and
outward troubles which our sins have deserved . . . and
nothing but the hand of His pardoning mercy will unbind it.'

We cannot help recalling Proverbs 5:22: 'The evil deeds of
a wicked man ensnare him; the cords of his sin hold him fast.'
In a word, Jerusalem had become the victim of sins of her own
sowing. That is what always happens. Who are we that we
should be so impertinent as to imagine that it will be different
for us? Shall we play with sin and expect God's blessing? Shall
we continue in sin and calmly expect grace to abound? Shall
we walk in sin and expect still to be vessels fit for the Master's
use? Shall we make friends with sin and expect to shine like
stars in the world?

The Lord has visited His people in judgement

The dominant picture in verse 15 is that of the winepress. **'In
his winepress the Lord has trampled the Virgin Daughter of
Judah.'** The treading of the winepress is a familiar Bible picture for the execution of divine judgement,[1] with all that goes
with it in terms of deliverance into enemy hands and the
people's great hopes and trusts, **'the warriors ... my young
men'**, left impotent.

The Lord has put his people to grief

What a sad verse is verse 16 – the eyes overflowing with tears,
the absence of any comforters, the deflated and cheerless
spirits and the children taken into captivity! What price now
the pleasures of sin for a season? **'My eyes overflow with tears'**
is literally 'my eye, my eye ...' Such an emphatic repetition of

the same word is not infrequent with Jeremiah (he does it with
'anguish', Jeremiah 4:19; 'peace', 6:14; 8:11; and 'a dream',
23:25, for example).

Five times in chapter 1 (1:2,9,16,17,21) there is an allusion
to the absence of a comforter, which some take as an allusion
to God the Holy Spirit. Certainly the twin phrases, **'No one is
near to comfort me, no one to restore my spirit'**, with their
echoes of Psalm 23:3, 'He restores my soul,' would seem to
give weight to this. It was the absence of God, who alone can
comfort His people with true comfort by His Word and His
Spirit, that Jerusalem deplored. She might have expressed
her grief as in Psalm 10:1: 'Why, O Lord, do you stand afar
off? Why do you hide yourself in times of trouble?' Listen to
Matthew Henry once more: 'God is the comforter; He used to
be so to her; He only can administer effectual comforts; it is
His word that speaks them; it is His Spirit that speaks them to
us. His are strong consolations, able to relieve the soul, to
bring it back when it is gone, and we cannot of ourselves fetch
it again; but now He has departed in displeasure ... It is no
marvel that the souls of the saints faint away, when God, who
is the only Comforter that can relieve them, keeps at a distance.' This we know: how our sin grieves the Holy Spirit, for
He is the Spirit of holiness. And when He is grieved, then we
are put to grief.

> What peaceful hours I once enjoyed!
>   How sweet their memory still!
> But they have left an aching void
>   The world can never fill.
>
> Return, O holy Dove! return,
>   Sweet messenger of rest!
> I hate the sins that made Thee mourn,
>   And drove Thee from my breast.
>
>   (William Cowper).

The Lord has left His people unclean

**'Zion stretches out her hands, but there is no one to comfort
her'** (1:17). This stretching out of the hands presents a most
pathetic picture. It is a token of the greatest distress and

extremity. Will no one take any notice? Will no one come to help? Doesn't anyone feel any sympathy or compassion? No one! The picture is of absolute despair. All hope has gone. **'The Lord has decreed for Jacob that his neighbours become his foes.'** Again, do you notice the emphasis upon the Lord's doing? As Calvin observes, 'The prophet again reminds us that the evils did not happen through men, but that God had resolved in this manner to punish the obstinate impiety of His people.'

The final part of the verse is the worst of all: **'Jerusalem has become an unclean thing among them.'** What is the great abiding charge from God to His people? 'But just as he who called you is holy, so be holy in all you do; for it is written, "Be holy, because I am holy"' (1 Peter 1:15-16, with roots in Leviticus). Again and again the call comes through to abstain from all forms of filthiness and uncleanness and to pursue righteousness and true holiness. John exhorts: 'Dear children, keep yourselves from idols' (1 John 5:21). James urges the need to 'keep oneself from being polluted by the world' (James 1:27). Paul reminds us: 'For God did not call us to be impure, but to live a holy life' (1 Thessalonians 4:7). Holiness, cleanliness, separation: these need to be the Christian's watchwords! But how often are they?

The excited speech which began in the second part of verse 11 ends with verse 16, as if the people were overcome by sheer exhaustion and cannot utter another word. 'Jeremiah breaks in on the lamentation of the city, as if the voice of the weeping one were choked with tears: thus he introduces into the complaint a suitable pause, that both serves to divide the lamentation into two and also brings a turn in its contents.'[2]

It certainly does! Look what it all leads up to!

What the Lord's people have done

Verse 18 begins with the magnificent statement: **'The Lord is righteous.'** The Hebrew word order is literally (and significantly): 'Righteous, He, Jehovah.' What a true and necessary acknowledgement! Absolute justice, righteousness, fairness, wisdom and perfection characterize all God's ways. If we are ever in doubt about that, then we need to heed the testimony of Abraham, the friend of God (Genesis 18:25) and Job, the blameless and upright one (Job 1:20-22; 40:1-5).

In making this declaration in verse 18, the people of God are admitting, by plain implication, that they have no grounds for complaint, no reason to suggest unfair treatment, and no further facts or extenuating circumstances that need to be taken into account. All is fair. All is just. All is right.

Now, sadly, it is repeatedly the tendency of the disobedient child of God to add to his own sin by seeking excuse or justification for it, or wanting to enter a plea in his own defence. But here we are glad to see there is none of that. And when it comes to unbelievers, then, of course, it is always everyone's fault except their own, and, with supreme irony, they are so very ready to blame the God whose very existence they question or deny for most of the rest of the time! But here the people recognize and freely admit that the fault is fairly and squarely on their part alone. **'The Lord is righteous, yet I rebelled against his command.'** It is the people's rebellion, the people's lawlessness, the people's disobedience, the people's unfaithfulness, which have led directly to all the sufferings and agonies that have already been described and that are gone into further in the remainder of the chapter. All of this underlines the unmistakable Bible truth that sin does not pay. Rebellion will not go unpunished. Our disobedience returns upon our own head. God will not be mocked – ever! And so the people own up.

In this present context, let us review what the sins of the people led to. There was *suffering*(1:12), real pain and agony. There was *sorrow* (1:16), genuine misery and heartbreak. There was *uncleanness* (1:17), (the AV translation, 'Jerusalem is as a menstruous woman among them', catches the awfulness of it all). Calvin remarks that Jerusalem was regarded by her enemies 'as offscourings, as an abominable filth'.

There was *exile* (1:18), with all the miserable separation and sundering involved there and, once again, the great hopes for the future gone – the **'young men and maidens'**. In saying '...yet I rebelled against his command', Henry observes that 'She owns the equity of God's actions, by owning the iniquity of her own.' Deviation from the Word of God is invariably at the root of the church's, and the Christian's,

problems. Again and again we are guilty of multiple unfaithfulness to the Word of God. And when this is so, God does
not stand idly by, doing nothing. Think of His intervention in
the early hours of the morning on Monday, 9 July 1984 in the
York Minster fire.

'Now if such a thing happened to the ancient church, let us
not wonder if at this day also God should deal with us more
severely than we wish. It is, indeed, a very bitter thing to see
the church so afflicted as to have the ungodly exulting over its
calamities, and that God's children should be as the refuse
and filth of the world. But let us patiently bear such a condition; and when we are thus contemptuously treated by our
enemies, let us know that God visits us with punishment, and
that the wicked do nothing except through the providence of
God, for it is His will to try our faith, and thus to show Himself
a righteous judge: for if we rightly consider in how many ways
and how obstinately we have provoked His wrath, we shall
not wonder if we also be counted at this day an abomination
and a curse.'[3]

> Lord, be Thy word my rule,
> In it may I rejoice;
> Thy glory be my aim,
> Thy holy will my choice.

>   (Christopher Wordsworth).

There was *betrayal* (1:19), with Israel's allies (AV, 'lovers')
no longer coming to the aid of the southern kingdom when the
Babylonian armies devastated the land. In consequence, **'My
priests and my elders perished in the city'** – famine took hold
of those men who had taken no notice of Jeremiah's warnings
about the false prophets and their lies, and they ended up, in
Harrison's striking phrase, 'finally dropping dead in their
tracks while looking for food'.

There was *torment* (1:20), a deep and felt torment of body
and spirit. For **'in my heart I am disturbed'**, the AV has 'my
bowels are troubled.' The bowels or intestines were regarded
as the seat of the emotions, and so emotional turmoil would
often be described in terms of bowel disturbances. The heart
was regarded as the seat of the intelligence and the will. Some
derive the word here in verse 20 from that for an ass, and render

it 'bound', as when a burden is fastened on an ass. Calvin, in contrast, derives it from a word for mortar or cement – just as cement is made by mixing water with lime and sand, stirring them together, so by a metaphor the bowels are said to be stirred or troubled. What is signified in the present case, of course, is the distress which arises from a disturbed conscience. There is no greater pain than that which wounds the conscience with the sting of sin.

And there was *dishonour* being brought upon the name of the Lord: **'All my enemies have heard of my distress; they rejoice at what you have done'** (1:21).

Before we leave this section, notice carefully how the character of God is used by the people here as the basis for pleading before Him. They appeal to His *mercy,* for that is what lies behind the language of verse 20, and prompts from Matthew Henry this comment: 'It is a matter of comfort to us that the troubles which oppress our spirits are open before God's eye' – even, we may add, when we have no one but ourselves to blame for all those troubles!

They also appeal to His *justice* (1:21-22). Undergirding the cry, **'May you bring the day you have announced so that they may become like me...deal with them as you have dealt with me because of all my sins,'** is not vindictive or self-righteous passion, but the cry of faith to God that, in His justice and for His own glory's sake, His name's sake, His Zion's sake, He would put down His enemies underneath his feet. There is no contradiction between such an appeal on the one hand and, on the other, obedience to the scriptural injunction to love, pray for and forgive our (and so the Lord's) enemies. Meditate in this connection upon Matthew 5:43-48, Romans 12:14-21 and Revelation 6:9-11.

There is a helpful remark in Lange's commentary: 'Here the question occurs, whether we may pray against our enemies, since Christ says, "Love your enemies"? Answer: There are two kinds of enemies. Some, who bear ill-will towards us personally for private reasons, concern ourselves alone. When the matter extends no further than to our own person, then should we privately commit it to God, and pray for those who are ill-disposed towards us, that God would bring them to a sense of their sin; and, besides, we ought, according to the injunction of Christ, to do them good, and not return evil for evil, but rather overcome evil with good. But if our enemies are not of that sort, that they bear ill-will towards us not for any private cause but on account of matters of faith; and are also opposed not only to us but especially to God in heaven, are fighting against His holy Word and are striving with eager impiety to destroy the Christian church – then indeed should we pray that God would convert those who may be converted, but as for those who continue ever to rage, stubbornly and maliciously, against God and His church, that God would execute upon them according to His own sentence judgement and righteousness (Psalm 139:19).'

A concluding word of application on 1:12-22

How salutary is the blow when God punishes a man for his sins here in this life, and by way of that punishment preserves him from the future, eternal and terrible wrath of God and from unquenchable hell fire! That holds good for both unbelievers and believers. It is true for unbelievers. Many of God's punishments (including many of 'life's disasters') prove ultimately to be of eternal benefit. By them, men have brought home to them a knowledge of their sins that they would not otherwise have attained, and some (though, sadly, only some) are brought to repentance and faith.

Think of it this way, if you like. While the leaves are on the trees you cannot see the birds' nests, but when all the leaves are off the trees in winter you can see them plainly. In a similar way, while men are in prosperity and 'have their leaves on' they fail to see what nests of ignorance, rebellion, lust and sin are filling their hearts and lives – they are blind and deceived. 'There is a way that seems right to a man, but in the end it leads to death' (Proverbs 14:12). But when their leaves are off in the day of affliction, they are enabled to see things more clearly and are brought to their senses (Luke 15:17). Maybe such have been God's dealings with you. It was not, perhaps, until illness, bereavement, financial loss or something else that you faced up to your sinfulness before God, saw the peril your soul was in, and were brought to that place and attitude of acknowledging the need to 'turn to God in repentance and have faith in our Lord Jesus' (Acts 20:21).

And the same principle is true for believers. Many a Christian can now say, 'It was good for me to be afflicted so that I might learn your decrees' (Psalm 119:71). Augustine recorded this prayer in his famous confessions: 'Lord, burn me here, saw me in pieces here, pierce me here, stone me here. Only spare me in that world.' And John Newton, in a magnificent hymn, captures it so well:

> I asked the Lord that I might grow
>   In faith, and love, and every grace,
> Might more of His salvation know,
>   And seek more earnestly His face.
>
> 'Twas He who taught me thus to pray,
>   And He, I trust, has answered prayer;
> But it has been in such a way
>   As almost drove me to despair.
>
> I hoped that in some favoured hour
>   At once He'd answer my request;
> And, by His love's constraining power,
>   Subdue my sins, and give me rest.
>
> Instead of this, He made me feel
>   The hidden evils of my heart,
> And let the angry powers of hell
>   Assault my soul in every part.
>
> Yea, more, with His own hand He seemed
>   Intent to aggravate my woe,
> Crossed all the fair designs I schemed,
>   Blasted my gourds, and laid me low.
>
> 'Lord, why is this? 'I trembling cried,
>   'Wilt Thou pursue Thy worm to death?'
> ''Tis in this way', the Lord replied,
>   'I answer prayer for grace and faith.

'These inward trials I employ
   From self and pride to set thee free,
And break thy schemes of earthly joy,
   That thou mayest seek thy all in Me.'

God's Word puts it very plainly: 'And you have forgotten that word of encouragement that addresses you as sons: "My son, do not make light of the Lord's discipline, and do not lose heart when he rebukes you, because the Lord disciplines those whom he loves, and he punishes everyone he accepts as a son"' (Hebrews 12:5-6). The order of things must always be – first the suffering, and then the glory! The Lord is righteous!

3.
Then and now

Please read Lamentations 2:1-9

The French have a phrase for it. They call it *déjà vu* – that sense of familiarity, of having been there before. And you might very well get that feeling as you come to chapter 2 of the book of Lamentations, for the same note continues to be struck. Even the first word is the same as it was in the first chapter, as if the second chapter is going to be a case of similar words set to the same tune. And so it is. The momentousness of what has happened demands it. But there is here no tedious repetition for the sake of it. Such difference as there is arises from the fact that chapter 1 focuses upon the opposed, helpless and comfortless condition of Jerusalem, while the main feature of the second chapter is the judgement which the Lord, in His wrath, has decreed against Jerusalem and Judah.

As we look at the first nine verses, we can distinguish three implied contrasts between 'then and now', between how things used to be and how they have now become. Indeed, the very first verse headlines all three.

God's relationship to His people

Stop and consider. Who is being spoken of in these verses? With whom is the Lord God having dealings? **'The Daughter of Zion'** (2:1), **'the Daughter of Judah'** (2:2) – in other words, His own people, those to whom He spoke the famous words: 'You only have I chosen of all the families of the earth' (Amos 3:2). Here are God's covenant people. That verse reminds the people that God's covenant with them is all of pure, free grace. We are reminded of John 15:16: 'You did not choose

me, but I chose you'; and 1 John 4:10: 'not that we loved God,
but that he loved us.' Yet this same verse from Amos gives no
excuse for sin. Indeed, in laying upon God's people the
covenant obligations, it contains the clear warning of punishment as a consequence of sin: 'You only have I chosen of all
the families of the earth; therefore I will punish you for all
your sins.' The covenant relationship, in which God says, 'I
will be their God, and they will be my people' (Jeremiah
31:33), lays upon those who belong to God very clear obligations to worship Him, obey Him, fear Him and love Him,
and to seek to walk blamelessly before Him in the way of His
commandments. The description of the godly man, who is
blessed, comes very much to mind (meditate carefully upon
Psalm 1:1-3).

There is a note of the incredibleness of it all in Jeremiah's
words here. 'For at the first sight it seemed very unreasonable
that a people whom God had not only received into favour,
but with whom He had made a perpetual covenant, should
thus be forsaken by Him,' observes Calvin. So how do we
account for the prophet's strong language and vigorous
expressions? Not by any suggestion that he meant to invali-
date God's faithfulness or constancy, but rather to arouse the
attention of the sleepy and slothful nation. An appalling hardness prevailed among the people, and Jeremiah desired that
it should be softened and that a humble and contrite spirit
should be implanted in them. This accounts for his exclam-
ation, in sheer astonishment: **'How the Lord has covered the
Daughter of Zion with the cloud of his anger!'**

Never, never, never are the people of God free (either then
or now, in those days or these) to argue, 'Shall we go on sinning, so that grace may increase?' The answer to such a suggestion is, and must always be, 'By no means! We died to sin;
how can we live in it any longer?' (Romans 6:1-2).

All of this is of direct importance to the passage in Lamentations which we have reached. Sin is bad enough under any
circumstances, committed by anyone, for it is an abomination
to God. But when sin is to be found among God's people,
against the covenant God, whose love and grace has been
known, tasted and experienced so richly, this heightens the
awfulness of the sin and the agony of its consequences. And

we see here how God deals not just with sinful people in general, but with His sinful people in particular.

Follow through and feel the weight of some of the phrases and statements here.

In verse 1 the prophet declares in amazement and wonder, 'How the Lord has covered the Daughter of Zion with the cloud of his anger!' Jeremiah sees a storm-cloud gathering over Jerusalem and shrouding everything in gloom. The word evidently signifies a thick cloud, or a black cloud. We cannot help thinking of the contrast with earlier days of God's dealings with His people, as our minds go back to the wonderful and memorable days of the Exodus. God's Word tells us that 'When Pharaoh let the people go, God did not lead them on the road through the Philistine country ... God led the people around by the desert road towards the Red Sea ... By day the Lord went ahead of them in a pillar of cloud to guide them on their way and by night in a pillar of fire to give them light . . . Neither the pillar of cloud by day nor the pillar of fire by night left its place in front of the people' (Exodus 13:17-22).

What happened when they reached the Red Sea and needed to cross it – with the Egyptian forces bearing down hard on them from behind, the desert wilderness stretching out uninvitingly on either side of them, and the Red Sea in front? We know the answer, of course. God divided the waters of the Red Sea so that the Israelites could walk across on dry ground. But notice this: 'Then the angel of God, who had been travelling in front of Israel's army, withdrew and went behind them. The pillar of cloud also moved from in front and stood behind them, coming between the armies of Egypt and Israel. Throughout the night the cloud brought darkness to the one side and light to the other; so neither went near the other all night long' (Exodus 14:19-20). Do you see that? The Egyptians were in the darkness on the one side of the cloud and the Israelites were in the light on the other side of the cloud.

God was a light to His people and He was darkness to His, and His people's, enemies. But, by way of stark contrast, God has now become a darkness to His people. The storm-cloud, the dark cloud, envelops not His enemies but His people! As Matthew Henry puts it, 'That side of the cloud is now turned towards them which was turned towards the Egyptians.' The divine anger is settling upon, of all people, 'the Daughter of Zion', filling the stoutest hearts with alarm and portending all manner of grievous things. No longer is it the cloud that led the Israelites from bondage to freedom. Rather it is a cloud of wrath sent to punish them for their aggravated abuse of that freedom. The anger of God is all the more terrible when manifested towards those who once enjoyed His favour and compassion. Remember Galatians 5:1,13: 'It is for freedom that Christ has set us free ... But do not use your freedom to indulge the sinful nature.'

Coming straight on to verse 2 for the moment, we learn that God is punishing His people **'without pity'**. The sense of that phrase is that He will not spare them. And in connection with this absence of pity the verb **'swallowed up'** is used. This verb is used several times in this section: 'The Lord has swallowed up all the dwellings of Jacob' (2:2); 'He has swallowed up Israel' (2:5); 'He has swallowed up all her palaces' (2:5). Moreover, as we continue to get a feel of this whole matter of the changes in God's relationship to His people the prophet uses a whole array of strong verbs to depict God's activity. 'He has torn down the strongholds of the Daughter of Judah. He has brought her kingdom and its princes down to the ground in dishonour' (2:2); 'He has cut off every horn of Israel. He has withdrawn his right hand at the approach of the enemy. He has burned in Jacob like a flaming fire' (2:3); 'He has strung his bow ... he has slain all who were pleasing to the eye ... he has poured out his wrath like fire' (2:4) And all of this is **'without pity'**, **'in his wrath'** (2:2) and **'in fierce anger'** (2:3).

And we must add, **'like an enemy ... like a foe'** (4:4). The covenant God like an enemy to His people? Like a foe to them? Has God changed? God cannot change! But God must punish sin, and since He is a jealous God, hating sin, compromise and rebellion in His people, He must punish them. Matthew Henry can help us: 'God is not really an enemy to His people, no, not when He is angry with them and corrects them in anger ... But sometimes He is "as an enemy" to them, when all His providences concerning them seem in outward appearance to have a tendency to their ruin, when everything makes against them and nothing for them.' All in all verse 4 is an amazing passage – and all that we have observed so far would be inconceivable, if it were not staggeringly true. That same divine power which in earlier and better days had accomplished mighty wonders for His covenant people has now been brought against His people for judgement. But there is no unfairness. Think back to 1:18: 'The Lord is righteous.' It is all a strict matter of just deserts.

The glory of Zion

The key statement is in verse 1: **'He has hurled down the splendour of Israel from heaven to earth.'** What is signified by the phrasé 'the splendour [AV, beauty] of Israel'? Surely it goes back to this: the glory of God's people is a reflection of His own glory. The covenant people of God is not just a motley crew of anybody and everybody. The church of God is distinctive, set apart, and cannot be compared with any other collection of people. Hence the fulness, dignity and variety in the description given of her in 1 Peter 2:9-10: 'But you are a chosen people, a royal priesthood, a holy nation, a people belonging to God, that you may declare the praises of him who called you out of darkness into his wonderful light. Once you were not a people, but now you are the people of God; once you had not received mercy, but now you have received mercy.' But there are also dangers – especially that of thinking we have laurels to rest upon, as if to say, 'Well, we are the covenant people of God, we belong to the true church of God, so everything will be bound to be all right; nothing can possibly ever go wrong.'

So far as the scenario in Lamentations is concerned, 'The nation had imagined that it occupied a privileged position because it stood in covenant relationship with God, and was seemingly unaware that such a status involved important obligations in the moral and spiritual realm. Now her degradation was as sudden as it was complete, and reduced her in an embarrassing fashion to a level even below that of other peoples.'[1]

So God intervened in judgement. He removed His people's splendour and glory in this descriptive phrase of hurling it down from heaven to earth. And this picture is certainly a comprehensive one, covering the removal of military power, governing power, the power of resistance, the availability of divine aid and all spiritual life and blessing. Let us look at some of the details.

'**The Lord has swallowed up all the dwellings of Jacob**' (2:2). This refers to the city dwellings and country houses in which people lived, as well as the pasture grounds where nomadic people spread their tents and allowed their flocks to graze – and, indeed, any open and unprotected places. Moreover, '**He has torn down the strongholds of the Daughter of Judah.**' Here are all the supposedly impregnable fortresses and defences, along with the walls, ramparts, gates and bars. This links in with the various details that follow in verses 8-9: '**He made ramparts and walls lament; together they wasted away. Her gates have sunk into the ground; their bars he has broken and destroyed.**' The gates, for example, are spoken of as if they have just disappeared into the earth, sinking under their own weight. Everything that would contribute to the nation's defence and security has been removed. As a result, all is left open and exposed, at the mercy of the enemy.

'**He has brought her kingdom and its princes down to the ground in dishonour**' (2:2). The Lord no longer considers them worthy of the honours conveyed upon them. Indeed, they have gone into exile '**among the nations**' (2:9), and their palaces also have been swallowed up (2:5).

An important phrase in verse 3 is the one which records that the Lord '**has cut off every horn of Israel**'. The horn is a familiar Old Testament symbol for strength. The Lord has left His people strengthless, resistless and helpless in the face of His wrath and their enemies. In their pride the people had lifted up their horn against God, so He has cut it off. We are reminded of the abiding truth that 'Apart from me you can do nothing' (John 15:5). Indeed there is a progress to a climax in verses 3-4. The cutting off of the horn, as we have seen, signifies the removal of the people's power, authority and influence, along with the power of resistance. The next statement takes things a stage further, for the withdrawal of God's '**right hand**' (the 'right hand' speaks of protection) means that His help has gone. To add to this, the burning and consuming at the end of verse 3, along with the description of the enemy with the bow all ready and strung at the beginning of verse 4, give a picture of God's positive and active hostility towards His sinful people. The bow, says Calvin, includes every other weapon. The part is stated for the whole. So when we are told that God **'has strung his bow'**, it is the same thought as though it was said that God was fully armed. He who was wont to defend His people has now taken up arms against them.

But another thing of great importance requires our notice. Has all this happened by chance? Is it just that everything has fallen out this way? The answer is in verse 8. **'The Lord determined...'**, we are told. He determined to do it. He purposed to do it. And what God purposes, He performs. This is underscored in the further statement that **'He stretched out a measuring line and did not withhold his hand from destroying.'** An architect and a builder use a measuring line in order to be as precise as possible in the matters of design and construction. Similarly, God set about this work of demolition and judgement with systematic thoroughness and exact attention to detail. The exactness of it, the deliberateness of it, the particularity of it are what is being stressed. And who can stand before Him?

Not only the sinful people themselves, but their dwellings, their goods, their plots of ground, their munitions and their governments are scourged by the wrath of God. Addressing himself to believers, the writer to the Hebrews insists, 'For our "God is a consuming fire"' (Hebrews 12:29). *'Our God'* – the God of His own people.

And what is the result of all this? **'He has multiplied mourning and lamentation for the Daughter of Judah'** (2:5).

Two words, both derived from the same Hebrew root and having a similar sound, are used to express the manifold and intense sorrows which had been experienced. Here is a most salutary lesson for us to learn. 'When our miseries come upon us from our enemies, we are not surprised ... when we can trace them as a direct result of our own folly and sin, we know they are deserved... but when the truth dawns upon us that God is against us, and it is His hand that smites us, we are shattered at the discovery, and our distress is unspeakably increased.'[2] Indeed it is. It is surely a most bitter ingredient in our sufferings when we are disobedient, to know that we have provoked the anger of our God – the God of covenant love.

The spiritual life of the people of God

Spiritual life is 'of the essence' where the people of God are concerned. We are a spiritual people who are to 'live by the Spirit' and 'keep in step with the Spirit' (Galatians 5:25), and who, if we would be 'the kind of worshippers the Father seeks … must worship in Spirit and in truth' (John 4:23-24). And Scripture warns us very firmly against 'having a form of godliness but denying its power' (2 Timothy 3:5).

The trouble for Judah was that she had neither form nor power. The power had been taken away. In no way was God any longer enthroned upon the praises of His people or manifesting Himself in the congregation of the righteous. But the form had all gone too. There was nothing left at all! The whole business of spiritual life and religious observance was in a state of complete wreckage.

The nub of the matter is, once more, stated in verse 1: **'He has not remembered his footstool in the day of his anger.'** We are familiar with God's statement in Isaiah 66:1: 'Heaven is my throne, and the earth is my footstool,' reminding us of the absolute sovereignty and omnipotence of God. But in our present verse the thought is rather of God's presence with His people. And in this sense God's 'footstool' is closely related to the ark of the covenant. A glance at 1 Chronicles 28:2 will establish this: 'King David rose to his feet and said: "Listen to me, my brothers and my people. I had it in my heart to build a house as a place of rest for the ark of the covenant of the Lord, for the footstool of our God, and I made plans to build it."' With that verse, compare Psalm 99:5 and Psalm 132:7-8. The ark of the covenant is that great symbol of God's presence where the mercy-seat was found, where God met with His people. As such it was most sacred. The cherubim stood over the cover of the ark (the mercy-seat) and as God spoke 'from between the two cherubim' (Numbers 7:89) and 'above the cover' (Exodus 25:22), it is not at all surprising to find the ark referred to as His footstool.

But we read that God 'has not remembered His footstool'. He put it aside. It fell, no doubt, into the hands of the invading Babylonians, as in an earlier day it had fallen into the hands of the Philistines (1 Samuel 4-5). Nothing could demonstrate God's anger against sin more vividly and force-fully than this. The greatest aspect of the splendour of Israel (God's presence with His people to bless them) was gone, both in symbol and reality. 'Of what little value are the tokens of His presence when His presence is gone!'[3]

Then verse 6 takes us to God's **'dwelling'** and **'his place of meeting'**. We are probably correct to take 'his dwelling' (AV, 'tabernacle') as referring to the temple.[4] But God has laid it waste (the verb carries the sense of acting with violence). Just as you might dismantle a garden shed or bulldoze a building, God demolished His temple. And, of necessity, **'He has destroyed his place of meeting.'** The people had provoked God to withdraw, and He withdrew.

Next to be mentioned are **'her appointed feasts and her Sab-baths'** (2:6). We saw the sadness of the abandoned feasts and festivals in 1:4. They were forgotten. No longer were their days marked out on the calendar or looked forward to and prepared for with great anticipation among the people of God.

But notice the special mention of 'her Sabbaths'. These also had been forgotten. The weekly observance of the Sabbath goes back, of course, to the fourth commandment: 'Remember the Sabbath day by keeping it holy. Six days you shall labour and do all your work, but the seventh day is a Sabbath to the Lord your God' (Exodus 20:8-10). The emphasis is upon the holiness and distinctiveness of that day. Behind the fourth commandment (as it itself makes clear) is the original creation ordinance of Genesis 2:1-3. That is why the Sabbath principle is a law for the *nation* and not only for the *church*. The law is cemented for all time, the one day in seven, although following the resurrection of the Lord Jesus Christ the day has changed. It is now 'the Lord's Day', the first day of the week (1 Corinthians 16:2; Revelation 1:10). But the whole principle of a Sabbath day of rest and consecration to God is unaffected in its nature by the change of day. Someone has said, 'Abolish the sabbath and the decay of religion begins.' Too true!

Think for a moment of the Sabbaths pictured in Isaiah 58:13-14:

'"If you keep your feet from breaking the Sabbath
    and from doing as you please on my holy day,
if you call the Sabbath a delight
    and the Lord's holy day honourable,
and if you honour it by not going your own way
    and not doing as you please or speaking idle words,
then you will find your joy in the Lord,
    and I will cause you to ride on the heights of the land
    and to feast on the inheritance of your father Jacob."
                    The mouth of the Lord has spoken.'

And put beside it this magnificent Puritan statement: 'The
Sabbath day is God's market day for the week's provision,
wherein He will have us come unto Him, and buy of Him
without silver or money, the Bread of Angels, and Water of
Life, the Wine of the Sacraments, and Milk of the Word to
feed our souls: tried gold to enrich our faith: precious eye
salve, to heal our spiritual blindness: and the white raiment of
Christ's righteousness to cover our filthy nakedness.'[5] It
should be heaven once a week!

How much of God's displeasure with *us*, both as a nation
and a church, in these days is linked to the continual and
increasing desecration of the Lord's Day, so that it becomes
increasingly difficult to distinguish it from any other day of
the week!

The 'Keep Sunday Special' campaign is well named! The
point is clearly established here in Lamentations: if God's
Sabbaths are not valued and observed as they should be, then
He Himself will deprive us of the benefit of them. Notice,
'The Lord has made Zion forget' (2:6).

There then follows God's spurning of **'both king and priest'**
(2:6), with which we may connect the opening sentence of
verse 7: **'The Lord has rejected his altar and abandoned his
sanctuary.'** The king and priest 'were as two pledges of God's
paternal favour', remarks Calvin. The kingdom was a mark of
God's favour for the people's defence and the priesthood was
to them the means by which reconciliation to God was
obtained. It was in the person of the Lord Jesus Christ Himself that the two offices were combined in a unique way.
When the prophet Zechariah speaks of One who 'will be a
priest on his throne' (Zechariah 6:13), it is to Christ that he

points and of Christ that he speaks. Christ is our King and Priest. So when God disregarded king and priest it became very evident 'that He was greatly displeased with His people, having thus, in a manner, obliterated His favours'.[6]

And with king and priest spurned, God's altar was rejected and His sanctuary abandoned. God no longer accepted the worship and the appointed sacrifices of His people; as we have seen, this was demonstrated anyway by the fact that the feasts were forgotten and the priests had been carried off into exile. What a tragic note is struck at the end of verse 7! The very temple area itself had been taken over by the enemy so that their celebratory shouts of victory over God's people are now heard on the feast days, instead of the worship and praises of God's people ascending to heaven to His glory. What, once more, of all those churches in our day that are now warehouses, mosques or derelict sites? A very different shout goes up. No longer is it 'a sacrifice of praise' to God, 'the fruit of lips that confess his Name' (Hebrews 13:15); and God is no longer glorified.

Which leaves the law and the prophets. They are brought before us in verse 9. **'The law is no more,'** records Jeremiah here. There were no longer any people to read it or any scribes to expound and teach it. The whole law, moral, ceremonial and judicial, so far as its administration in Judah is concerned, was no more. The actual tables of the law from Sinai were housed in the ark of the covenant, but the ark, too, was gone. There was 'a famine of hearing the words of the Lord' (Amos 8:11). And that being the case, we are not surprised to find that **'Her prophets no longer find visions from the Lord.'** It does not mean that there were no prophets and no prophecy, or that every prophet was a false prophet, but rather that when Jerusalem was destroyed there were no more revelations from God, no more divine communications, no more words from the Lord for Judah's relief, help, comfort, encouragement or deliverance from her present sorrows.

The law is the summary of the rule of life given by God to His people. In this connection, the statement from the Puritan Samuel Bolton is as important as it is memorable: 'The law sends us to the Gospel for our justification; the Gospel sends us to the law to frame our way of life.'[7] And prophecy was the constant witness of the activity of the living God among His people. By these means – the law and the prophets – the Lord sought to conduct His people to the object of their election and calling and to fit them for becoming a holy nation and a kingdom of priests. But 'The law is no more, and her prophets no longer find visions from the Lord.' 'They had persecuted God's prophets and despised the visions they had from the Lord, and therefore it is just with God to say that they shall have no more prophets, no more visions. Let them go to the prophets that had flattered and deceived them with visions of their own hearts, for they shall have no more from God to comfort them, or tell them how long.'[8]

This is an abiding principle with God, and there have been many illustrations of it down the centuries all the way to our own day. If God's people despise His Word, God is careful to punish them by taking that Word away. The curse which they choose comes to them, and the blessing they do not choose is taken from them. 'Where there is no vision, the people perish' (Proverbs 29:18,AV). God was silent.

So, with the buildings destroyed, the defences removed, the religious observances forgotten, the rulers in exile, the law no more and the prophets no longer announcing or ministering the Word of the Lord – surely the ruin of God's people was complete.

What, then, shall we say in response to this? What is the central application of this section for us?

All the time I have been writing and rewriting this chapter some words from Peter's first letter have been weighing upon me, and they give the clue for our final application before moving on: 'For it is time for judgement to begin with the family of God; and if it begins with us, what will the outcome be for those who do not obey the gospel of God? And "If it is hard for the righteous to be saved, what will become of the ungodly and the sinner?"' (1 Peter 4:17-18).

God's judgement upon Judah and Jerusalem is surely a solemn warning for us. While we recognize that 'Not all who are descended from Israel are Israel' (Romans 9:6), that not every single member of the 'nation' belonged to the 'church', yet surely some very sober reflections should be prompted in our hearts.

Let me put it this way.

If God, the righteous Judge, so hates evil and must deal with it that He judges His redeemed people, what will be the fate of unbelievers when His full wrath against sinners is revealed?

If even the children of God, the objects of His special covenant love, are severely chastised for their sins, what can the godless expect at the last day?

If even the best and holiest of God's servants have so much amiss in them that renders it necessary for God to correct and punish them, then what is the prospect for those who are his enemies?

If the justified sinner who is seeking with all earnestness and perseverance to live a life that is pleasing to God faces God's judgements and censures, then what will become of the empty formalist with his ceremonies, the false professor with his hypocrisy, the proud sinner with his presumption or the barrenly orthodox with his creed?

If even the true coin is severely tested, what will become of the reprobate silver?

If God has to visit us with punishments, corrections and disciplines which are absolutely just and necessary, because of our unstable and unwary walking, our self-pleasing and earthliness, our relish for the things of this passing world, our forgetting of our spiritual inheritance and our heavenly home, our conforming ourselves to the world, then what will become of the Christless and the wicked, however much they may delude themselves for the time being with the appearance of things that they are flourishing freely in the world and are getting away with everything they do?

If the righteous are only saved with difficulty, what will be the end of those who are not saved at all?

Make sure that you are covered with Christ's righteousness, and led by God's Spirit into the *ways* of righteousness. 'Therefore, my brothers, be all the more eager to make your calling and election sure' (2 Peter 1:10).

4.
The wages of sin

Please read Lamentations 2:10-22

Following the account we have just been given of the anger of Zion's God, we are now faced with the mournful picture of the sorrow of Zion's children. This section shows us even more clearly the appropriateness of the title 'Lamentations' for this book of Scripture. The whole is shot through with lamentation, mourning and despair. Moreover, there is a clear feeling in these verses that we have here the language of an eyewitness, and this heightens the atmosphere. The picture painted could not be more vivid. It is just as if we were there ourselves to gaze upon the awful scene.

The characters of lamentation

On every side the people were in agony and woe. The first to be mentioned are **'the elders of the Daughter of Zion'** (2:10). Their grief is too deep for words; they just **'sit on the ground in silence'**.

Who are these elders? Back in the days of the patriarchs the title would probably be used to refer to heads of families. The word occurs in Numbers 11:25 to describe the seventy men on whom the Spirit rested, who were appointed to assist Moses in judging and ruling the people. During the days when the people of Israel were settling into the land of Canaan, each city had its own elders who controlled local affairs. In terms of the reference here in Lamentations we could probably best describe them as judges and magistrates.

But what a contrast is presented! They were accustomed to sit with dignity on the judgement seats, the 'thrones of the house of David', and at the city gates in their royal robes, weighing the evidence and making their pronouncements. But no longer! They now 'sit on the ground in silence'. And their character as mourners is emphasized by the reference to dust and sackcloth: **'They have sprinkled dust on their heads.'** This was a characteristic expression of sorrow and grief. Classic Old Testament examples can be found in Joshua 7:6, following the defeat of the Israelites at Ai because of the sin of Achan; Job 2:12, when Job's three 'friends' first saw him in his affliction; and Ezekiel 27:30, in the course of the lament for Tyre. And they have **'put on sackcloth'.** This spoke in the same way of having experienced great calamity and so having been brought into great grief. People would wear sackcloth when mourning for the dead: for example, the patriarch Jacob put it on when mourning for his son Joseph who had been reported killed. They would put on sackcloth when convicted before God of their sin: the inhabitants of Nineveh expressed their repentance in this way after God had blessed the preaching of Jonah to their souls. And sackcloth – which was black and usually made from goat's hair – was also worn as a sign of grief for personal or national disaster. Mordecai, in the book of Esther, wore sackcloth when he heard of Haman's plot to destroy the Jews and the edict that had been issued.

But the elders did not lament alone. **'The young women of Jerusalem have bowed their heads to the ground'** (2:10). No more songs, no more timbrels, no more dancing, no more 'walking along with outstretched necks, flirting with their eyes, tripping along with mincing steps, with ornaments jingling on their ankles' (Isaiah 3:16). Their pride has been humbled, their joy has been removed, their prospects have been shattered, their popularity has vanished. They have been brought down to the ground.

And there was another who lamented also – the prophet Jeremiah himself. He expresses his own agony and anguish most movingly and effectively in verse 11. He confesses himself to be absolutely exhausted with grief because everything seems so heavy and hopeless. **'My eyes fail from weeping,'** he says. As Matthew Henry observes, 'He has wept till he can weep no more, has almost wept his eyes out, wept himself blind.' **'I am in torment within,'** Jeremiah goes on – the same phrase we had in 1:20 signifying acute emotional disturbance. For 'heart', the AV has 'liver', as the verse continues, **'My heart is poured out on the ground.'** The liver is the heaviest organ of the human body and was understood traditionally to be associated with depressive and melancholic disorders. What Jeremiah is saying, in effect, is that the sharpness of his sorrow is such that his feelings are entirely giving way under it; everything is really too much for him to bear; he can no longer hold himself back in restraint; he is overwhelmed with sorrow. The result is that he is exhausted. But over what? **'Because my people are destroyed.'**

The causes of lamentation

One by one the prophet takes us through the destruction of those whom he so feelingly describes as 'my people'. We can discern five features, the fifth being 'behind' the whole array.

First, there is *famine*. The second part of verse 11 and the whole of verse 12 paint a terrible word-picture of **'children and infants [fainting] in the streets of the city'**. They cried pathetically to their mothers for food and liquid refreshment: **'Where is bread and wine?'** The older ones staggered around **'like wounded men in the streets of the city'**, searching vainly for scraps of food. And, the most heart-rending picture of all, some of them in their hunger and faintness died as their mothers held them close: **'as their lives ebb away in their mothers' arms'**. We can picture some of this all the more realistically from the news reports we see on television. If this is not a harrowing picture, what is?

There is a similar note at the end of verse 19, as the children **'faint from hunger at the head of every street'**. There were dead and dying little ones to be met at every turn. And incredible as it may seem, some of the mothers were even driven to the cannibalism of eating **'their offspring, the children they have cared for'** (2:20). Earlier on, so Jeremiah 14 informs us, God had sought to correct His people through drought and famine, but they had not responded in repentance. A far, far greater degree of this extremity has, in consequence, now come upon them.

Secondly, there is *death by the sword*. No one was spared at the hands of the cruel Babylonian invaders. **'Priest and prophet ... young and old ... young men and maidens'** alike were killed (2:20-21). **'No one escaped or survived'** (2:22). There were, of course, multitudes who survived the slaughter and remained alive on the earth. Not every individual, literally, was killed. The point surely is that no one escaped entirely the effects of God's wrath. None were exempt from it. It came home, in one way or another, to all. All were involved in a common ruin. In respect of the opening of verse 21, someone has remarked, 'When general judgements proceed from God, the old and the young must suffer together: the old because they have not rightly educated the young: the young because they have imitated the wickedness of the old.' How supremely important are verses like Proverbs 22:6 and Ephesians 6:4!

And no place was considered sacred. The priests and prophets were **'killed in the sanctuary of the Lord'** (2:20). Even there blood was spilled. Harrison comments that those who 'with such callous frequency had debased the high spiritual traditions associated with their Lord's house, had now met their end at the scene of their crimes'. Bodies lay piled up on one another **'in the dust of the streets'** (2:21). Death stretched into home after home and affected family after family, so that Jerusalem, personified, could say, in the language of a mother speaking of her children, **'Those I cared for and reared, my enemy has destroyed'** (2:22). The same verse uses what appears to be the picture of a bird of prey hovering and encircling: **'As you summon to a feast day, so you summoned against me terrors on every side.'**

Thirdly, there are *the false prophets*. The true prophet, Jeremiah, does not mince his words about them in verse 14: **'The visions of your prophets were false and worthless; they did not expose your sin to ward off your captivity. The oracles they gave you were false and misleading.'** Why so? For the reason, of course, that they came from men and not from God. And how do we know this? Look again at the central statement of the verse. Jeremiah tells us that 'They did not expose your sin to ward off your captivity.' Consider one or two examples of what these false prophets had been saying. '"Peace, peace," they say, when there is no peace' (Jeremiah 6:14). 'The prophets keep telling them, "You will not see the sword or suffer famine. Indeed, I will give you lasting peace in this place"' (Jeremiah 14:13). The examples could be multiplied. During the period just preceding the overthrow of Judah there were a number of people who were accustomed to say, 'The burden of the Lord', but who were mere pretenders to divine visions. They gave chaff, not wheat. They made everything up. They followed their own fancies. They were interested only in themselves and their followings. They were those of whom the Lord Almighty said, 'I did not send these prophets, yet they have run with their message; I did not speak to them, yet they have prophesied' (Jeremiah 23:21, see also verse 22). The false prophets often declared boldly and brazenly that whatever Jeremiah said and threatened was of no account. They were prophets after their own hearts rather than after God's heart.[1]

There is a very important and necessary application here to the ministry of the Word in our own day. God no longer sends prophets, of course, with fresh revelations from Himself. He sends preachers, ministers of the Word, whose solemn task it is to declare the whole counsel of God, without fear or partiality. And that ministry must, of necessity, include, as a high profile, the declaring of the sinfulness of sin in general, as well as the putting of the finger upon particular sins and faults and offences in God's sight, and here the false prophets of our text failed lamentably and miserably and conspicuously. One reason, no doubt, why they neglected to do this is that they thought they would lose support, popularity, affection and a ready hearing. In that they may well have been correct, but it is not the consideration which should have motivated them. Far more important to be able to say, with the apostle Paul, 'So I strive always to keep my conscience clear before God and man' (Acts 24:16); and again, 'Therefore, I declare to you today that I am innocent of the blood of all men. For I have not hesitated to proclaim to you the whole will [AV, counsel] of God' (Acts 20:26-27). Another reason, no doubt, why the false prophets spoke as they did was that, as Matthew Henry puts it, 'They knew they could not reprove their hearers without reproaching themselves at the same time.'

The application to our own day stands out a mile. How often do we hear the nation's and the church's present turmoil and agonies exposed in the true way? There is nothing more necessary than that men be warned, so that, becoming conscious of our iniquities, we may repent. These false prophets of Jeremiah's day had corrupted the prophetic doctrine. They had not preached respecting the holiness and the vengeance of God. They had not exhorted the people to repentance. They had not bidden them to seek the mercy of God. And we see exactly the same. On crucial matters like the deity of the Lord Jesus Christ, His virgin birth, atoning death, literal resurrection, the necessity of the new birth and so on, voices are quiet or are spreading error abroad. On vital moral matters like homosexuality, adultery and abortion there is similar and utter failure to proclaim biblical truth. No longer are there clear statements abounding on the eternal reality of heaven and the equally eternal reality of hell. So many will not declare these things, because, of course, they do not believe them, and so if they were to proclaim them they would expose themselves.

We are surrounded by false prophets, false preachers, false teachers, who run, yet God has not sent them. They are liberals, modernists, atheists, humanists, evolutionists, existentialists, freemasons and everything else in the world – except the one thing they claim to be, namely, the spokesmen of God.

Listen to Calvin: 'Let us learn by this how to distinguish between the faithful servants of God and impostors. For the Lord by His Word summons us before His tribunal, and would have our iniquities discovered, that we may loathe ourselves, and thus open an entrance for mercy. But when what is brought before us only tickles our ears and feeds our curiosity, and, at the same time, buries all our iniquities, let us then know that the refined things which vastly please men are insipid and useless. Let, then, the doctrine of repentance be approved by us, the doctrine which leads us to God's tribunal, so that being cast down in ourselves we may flee to His mercy.'

God's punishment is a fearful thing, whoever is on the receiving end of it. But it must be peculiarly fearful when it comes upon those who, in the name of God, have led people astray by perverting His truth. By the same token, hell will be a terrible place for all who will be found in it. But it will be peculiarly terrible for those – including many of the fêted

'Christian leaders' of our own day, to say nothing of those from history – who, in the name of God, have been blind leaders of the blind, with the result that they will all have fallen into the pit. Is it any wonder that James declares in his letter, 'Not many of you should presume to be teachers, my brothers, because you know that we who teach will be judged more strictly'? (James 3:1).

Fourthly, there is *the inevitable scorn and derision from Judah's enemies*. This comes through potently in verses 15-16. Read those two verses carefully. God's people had become the latest joke in everyone's eyes. What gleeful, hand-rubbing, sickening gloating is witnessed in these verses! Jerusalem had had a great name. We have already observed 1:6 and 2:1. Now, as her enemies **'clap their hands'** and **'scoff and shake their heads'** – at whom? – 'at the Daughter of Jerusalem', listen to what they say: **'Is this the city that was called the perfection of beauty, the joy of the whole earth?'**

We cannot help thinking of Psalm 48 (the whole psalm, but look in particular at verses 1-3 and 12-13). And what of Psalm 50:2: 'From Zion, perfect in beauty, God shines forth'? What price Zion now? From being the envy and terror of all around, she is now the laughing-stock. The enemies' mouths are opened wide and they exult, saying, **'We have swallowed her up. This is the day we have waited for; we have lived to see it.'** They had for a long time been wishing and hoping. Now they were seeing. And the second part of verse 17 adds more of the same to the total picture: **'He has overthrown you without pity, he has let the enemy gloat over you, he has exalted the horn of your foes.'** It seems that the enemies of God and His people had got what they wanted. The whole scene puts us in mind of the scene around the Saviour's cross, and the vile satisfaction expressed by His enemies at what appeared to them to be their victory and His overthrow. Meditate for a moment prayerfully upon the following passages: Matthew 27:39-44; Mark 15:29-32; Luke 23:35-37.

There is a solemn truth here. The church and the world, the kingdom of light and the kingdom of darkness, are at war with one another. They are deadly enemies. And, as the book of Revelation demonstrates so clearly, this is only the outward and visible outworking of the conflict between the Lord Jesus Christ Himself and Satan. Much that goes on under the name

of 'the true church' is, of course, false, utterly false, carnal
rather than spiritual, and so offensive to God. But where the
true church of Christ is concerned, many a time her enemies
think they have got the better of her and begin to congratulate
themselves that the church is not only down but finally out.
This is pictured very vividly, for example, in Revelation 11:3-
13. But they make a major error. They have got it completely
wrong. For has not the Head of the church Himself said, 'I will
build my church, and the gates of Hades will not overcome
it'? (Matthew 16:18). At the end of the day the enemies of the
truth can clap their hands, scoff, hiss, wag their heads, curl
their lips, gnash their teeth and do anything else they like.
The true church of Christ is indestructible.

A word to any who might be on the receiving end of such
scoffing right now. Do not let it trouble you. It is the devil's
special delight to make a mockery of the church and all the
godly who belong to it. But do not let that ridicule ever cause
you to waver. God's call to us is to remain firm and faithful to
Him. And do not lose sight of Matthew 5:11-12: 'Blessed are
you when people insult you, persecute you and falsely say all
kinds of evil against you because of me. Rejoice and be glad,
because great is your reward in heaven, for in the same way
they persecuted the prophets who were before you.'
Remember, God can easily and speedily take away such
reproach, if it please Him, and put to silence the 'triumphing'
of the wicked. And, of course, on the last day He *will* do so for
good! Hallelujah!

I mentioned, with respect to the causes of lamentation, that
there were five features recorded here, and that the fifth is
'behind' the whole lot. We have seen four of these causes:
famine, death by the sword, the false prophets and the gleeful
scorn of Judah's enemies. But what lay behind each of these
features? The answer is: *the Lord*. This confirms what we
learned in the previous section (2:1-9).

The important passage now is the first part of verse 17. To
be sure, the Babylonians wrought much destruction. But – as
with Pilate in respect of Jesus (John 19:11) – they would have
had no power if it had not been given to them from above. So,
**'The Lord has done what he planned; he has fulfilled his word,
which he decreed long ago.'** 'Whatever are the calamities suffered, whatever the taunts to which the people are exposed in

their ruined condition, they have not come from the onslaught of ruthless foes, but from God, their own God.'[2] To which Matthew Henry adds, 'They [i.e. the foes] are but the sword in God's hand.' The second part of verse 17, which we have noticed already, merely underscores and confirms this. **'He has overthrown you without pity, he has let the enemy gloat over you, he has exalted the horn of your foes.'**

But notice that He has not acted without warning. He gave notice first. Jeremiah 18:11-12 shows that this is so, but we could go right back to Leviticus 26:14-45 or Deuteronomy 28:15-68. Spend a moment checking those passages out. God has merely – I say, merely – carried out His word. He has acted consistently with Himself, as He always does and always must. And to bring matters right up to date and, indeed, to project them into the future, this is why no one will be able to point a finger at God on the judgement day, when He separates the sheep from the goats, and says to the one, 'Come, you who are blessed by my Father; take your inheritance, the kingdom prepared for you since the creation of the world,' and to the other, 'Depart from me, you who are cursed, into the eternal fire prepared for the devil and his angels' (see Matthew 25:31-46). Here comes Matthew Henry once more: 'In all the providences of God concerning His church it is good to take notice of the fulfilling of His word; *for there is an exact agreement between the judgements of God's hand and the judgements of His mouth,* and when they are compared they will mutually explain and illustrate each other.' The same holds true in respect of His dealings with the world.

The cure for lamentation

There is a question in verse 13 and an answer in verses 18-19.

Look first at *the question Jeremiah asked.* Read verse 13. The opening query, **'What can I say for you?'** has the force of 'What comforts can I provide for you? What similar instances can I present for comparison with what has happened to you? What testimony can I bring to encourage you?' And the fact of the matter is that Jeremiah is left speechless. He has no comforting words to provide, no comparable incidents to quote, no encouraging testimonies to present. The case is unparalleled. Why? Because of the uniqueness and serious-ness of the situation facing Judah and Jerusalem. **'Your wound is as deep as the sea. Who can heal you?'** She faces a sea of miseries, a flood of troubles, an ocean of sorrow.

You know how it is. You might on occasions be in great dis-tress – yet you can compare your distress with that of others, you can take counsel and derive comfort from others who have been that way before and have gleaned appropriate lessons from their experience; you are conscious that others are in worse distress even than you. But none of that applied in Judah's case. She stood alone. There was no city that had been so highly privileged with divine honours. And there was no city which had been so signally punished. **'Look, O Lord, and consider: Whom have you ever treated like this?'** (2:20).

And in order, somehow, to get this across to Judah, Jeremiah uses the imagery of the raging sea beating its way through the sea wall and causing so radical a breach or wound that nothing can be done in the face of it. It was utterly beyond the wisdom or power of man with his schemes and brainwaves (and technologies!) to put things right and make things well and whole again. Human words failed. Human help was powerless. Human wisdom was futile.

Now turn to *the answer Jeremiah gave*. We find it in verses 18-19. To be sure, as has just been indicated, all human effort and ingenuity was vain in present circumstances. But what of the Lord? **'I am the Lord, the God of all mankind. Is anything too hard for me?'** (Jeremiah 32:27). 'With man this is imposs-ible, but not with God; all things are possible with God' (Mark 10:27). And so the true prophet turns the people's attention to the Lord, the only One who can help them.

What is the way back? It is, as it must always be, the way of godly sorrow and repentance. 'Godly sorrow brings repen-tance that leads to salvation and leaves no regret, but worldly sorrow brings death' (2 Corinthians 7:10). The first move is this: **'The hearts of the people cry out to the Lord'** (cf. Psalm 50:15). Their cry is not one of complaint but of grief and repentance. And what follows expresses a pleading with holy desire and expectation before God, with much earnestness and passion: **'O wall of the Daughter of Zion, let your tears flow like a river day and night.'**

Why is the wall addressed? It is not quite as surprising as it looks. We sometimes take the frontiers for the country of which they mark the boundary, the house for its inhabitants, or the purse for its contents. Here, in poetic imagery, the prophet seems to envisage the wall of the city embracing the city itself and its people. It had been for so long symbolic of their defence and protection and now he bids it shed tears on behalf of those whom it had sheltered. The pre-eminence of the wall may be seen from the fact that in Nehemiah's day everything depended upon its restoration. So if the 'wall of the Daughter of Zion' is taken for the Daughter of Zion herself, it is not so surprising that the same activities are attributed to the wall which belong properly to the people, and that the wall is exhorted to weep and pray for its children. Back in 1:4 we had 'The roads to Zion mourn,' and in 2:8 'Ramparts and walls lament.' Ultimately, then, Jeremiah is exhorting the people themselves and calling them to weep.

The phrase 'let your tears flow like a river' shows that no casual business, no play-acting is in mind or will suffice. It is true that some grief is too deep for tears. Yet, notwithstanding, a genuine grief will again and again express itself in tears – and, more often than not, needs to, for it cannot bottle itself up. We need only think of the Lord Jesus Christ at the grave of Lazarus (John 11:35) and weeping over Jerusalem (Luke 19:41). Since it is God who has wounded His people, it is God alone who must be called upon and entreated to heal them again. Man-made schemes, gimmicks and all the rest of it can never take the place of true repentance, the fear of the Lord, holiness and obedience. They never could. They never will. The only appeal of the helpless is to God Himself, who is not unmoved by the entreaties of His people who would call upon Him, and in calling upon Him would return to Him. A matchless passage upon this theme is Hosea 14. Have a look at it now.

There is a sense in all this, surely, of Psalm 85:4-7:

'Restore us again, O God our Saviour,
    and put away your displeasure towards us.
Will you be angry with us for ever?
    Will you prolong your anger through all generations?

Will you not revive us again,
    that your people may rejoice in you?
Show us your unfailing love, O Lord,
    and grant us your salvation.'

And Jeremiah further exhorts the people, '**Give yourself no
relief, your eyes no rest**' (literally, 'Let not the daughter [or
pupil] of your eye cease [or, be silent]' – perhaps because the
pupil is the tenderest part of the eye).

The call for continual crying to the Lord continues in verse
19, in two full and instructive statements. The first, '**Arise, cry
out in the night, as the watches of the night begin,**' reminds us
that there are certain things which are even more important
than rest and sleep. Being right with God is the most important of them; being right with one another arises out of that –
hence Ephesians 4:26: 'Do not let the sun go down while you
are still angry.' The night was divided into three watches of
four hours each. 'There are crises in life, times of trouble and
peril, when the time usually devoted to sleep may fitly be
employed in earnest, agonizing prayer. Such a time had come
in the history of Judah; such a time comes to most.'[3]Has it
come to us – on account of our own sins, the sins of the church
and the sins of the nation? 'My eyes stay open through the
watches of the night, that I may meditate on your promises'
(Psalm 119:148).

The second statement is the call: '**Pour out your heart like
water in the presence of the Lord.**' This is one of the most
striking and eloquent statements in the whole book of
Lamentations. It speaks of being serious and sincere in
prayer; of being free and full in prayer, holding nothing back;
of spreading your whole case before the Lord and casting
yourself unreservedly upon Him. This attitude is evidenced
further in the call: '**Lift up your hands to him for the lives of
your children.**' It is not so much the action of lifting the hands
as sufficient in itself which is intended here, as the prayer and
confidence in God which is symbolized and expressed by the
gesture.

'Prayer is a salve for every sore, even the sorest, a remedy
for every malady, even the most grievous. And our business
in prayer is not to prescribe, but to subscribe to the wisdom
and will of God; to refer our case to Him, and then to leave it

with Him,' says Matthew Henry. Surely that remains a word
in season to our souls.

> Come, let us to the Lord our God
>   With contrite hearts return;
> Our God is gracious, nor will leave
>   The desolate to mourn.
>
> His voice commands the tempest forth
>   And stills the stormy wave;
> And though His arm be strong to smite,
>   'Tis also strong to save.

(John Morison).

That famous verse, 2 Chronicles 7:14, is still true: 'If my
people, who are called by my name, will humble themselves
and pray and seek my face and turn from their wicked ways,
then will I hear from heaven and will forgive their sin and will
heal their land.'

5.
The rod of God's wrath

Please read Lamentations 3:1-18

This third chapter of Lamentations is quite remarkable. The sufferings of the people of Judah are described here in terms of the experience of a single individual. Jeremiah's feelings pour out in the light of God's displeasure upon the people and all the felt consequences of it. Matthew Henry suggests that the title prefixed to Psalm 102 would be an appropriate one to apply here: 'A prayer of an afflicted man. When he is faint and pours out his lament before the Lord.'[1]

The bulk of the chapter is in the first person, and cast in terms of God's dealings with a solitary individual and that individual's agonizing before God (note the use of 'I', 3:1-24; 'we', 3:22, 40-47, and the return to 'I', 3:48-66). But how are we to understand and interpret the chapter in terms of who is speaking and who is being spoken of? Clearly it is not every individual Jew who is speaking. Yet neither, as Laetsch observes, 'is it Jeremiah weeping in bitter grief over the injustices committed against him by his countrymen, their mockeries, their insults, their persecutions, particularly his imprisonment in the dungeon', and so on. Certainly we have here the language of personal sorrow, but Jeremiah is not making his own sufferings the subject of his complaint. Rather, he wrestles for his and, more importantly, God's people.

As we follow the present section through (3:1-18) we can isolate five separate aspects of the prophet's griefs and perplexities on the people's behalf.

1. God is against him

We have already seen how the people were very slow in grasping that the Lord their God was behind all that had been happening to them. Consequently the prophet has had to insist on this (e.g., 2:1,8,17). It was because of his own pure conscience and sensitive heart that Jeremiah could see these things so clearly and could recognize the fierce anger of the Lord against all the sins and evils which had corrupted the consciences and hearts of his fellow-countrymen. We cannot but be reminded of Jeremiah 8:21, which in the NIV reads, 'Since my people are crushed, I am crushed; I mourn, and horror grips me,' and in the AV is 'For the hurt of the daughter of my people I am hurt; I am black; astonishment hath taken hold on me.'

And so Jeremiah announces in verse 1, **'I am the man who has seen affliction by the rod of his wrath.'** The phrase 'the rod of his wrath' (the Lord is not actually mentioned by name until verse 18) sets the tone. It is always man's heaviest affliction to be under God's chastisement. But wait and remember. When God is angry with His people it is not an action in His hatred to destroy us but one in His love to correct us. This is drawn to our attention very clearly in the letter to the Hebrews. First the writer urges: 'Our fathers disciplined us for a little while as they thought best; but God disciplines us for our good, that we may share in his holiness. No discipline seems pleasant at the time, but painful. Later on, however, it produces a harvest of righteousness and peace for those who have been trained by it' (Hebrews 12:10-11). He then follows that up immediately with the vigorous practical exhortation of verse 12: 'Therefore, strengthen your feeble arms and weak knees!' Similarly the apostle Paul speaks in one breath of 'the kindness and sternness [AV, goodness and severity] of God' (Romans 11:22). There is no contradiction between them.

Indeed, and let us learn this lesson well, the most helpful feature of our afflictions and chastisements from the Lord is that very moment when we actually realize that it *is* the Lord who is afflicting and chastising us, and when, as a result, we are brought to a fresh consciousness of our sin, genuine repentance and a cry for forgiveness. 'Then it is that wrath gives place to mercy: punishment is disarmed by pardon.'[2]

The rod has a very important place, then, in God's gracious dealings with us. The very rod which is 'the rod of his wrath' (cf. Isaiah 10:5) is also the rod of His comfort and strength. It is part of the shepherd's pastoral equipment, we might say. Micah draws attention to this: 'Shepherd your people with your staff, the flock of your inheritance' (Micah 7:14). And so, of course, does the psalmist David in the matchless 23rd Psalm.

2. God appears to him as an enemy

We can summarize the next section (3:2-6) in this way. The prophet is walking in the dark (3:2-3), experiencing sore affliction in body and mind (3:4), and feels surrounded 'with bitterness and hardship' (3:5), like a man under siege. In this rock-bottom condition of dejection he feels like a gone-and-forgotten dead man (3:6) with no way out.

If we were to respond by suggesting that Jeremiah is becoming over-fanciful or melodramatic in his choice of language we would do him a great injustice. 'It is not possible sufficiently to set forth the greatness of the sorrow which the faithful feel when terrified by the wrath of God,' observes Calvin, and he is absolutely right. And these verses themselves underscore the appropriateness of Jeremiah – like no other – being the one who best personifies and feels uniquely the sorrows and sufferings, the afflictions and the extremities, of God's people at this time.

'He has driven me away and made me walk in darkness rather than light' (3:2). Darkness stands for great trouble and perplexity, the complete lack of comfort and direction, and the path of Jeremiah's life certainly often lay through darkness. His recollection of the miseries of his own imprisonment in the dungeon would have remained with him, as it would with anyone who had experienced such a thing (cf. Jeremiah 37:15-16; 38:6,10-13). Someone has commented that 'There is nothing so distressing, so oppressive, so bewildering, so hopeless to contend with, as darkness.' But the counsel of God to all such remains the same: 'Who among you fears the Lord and obeys the word of his servant? Let him who walks in the dark, who has no light, trust in the name of the Lord and rely on his God' (Isaiah 50:10).

The prophet continues, **'Indeed, he has turned his hand against me again and again, all day long'** (3:3). On this,

Matthew Henry remarks, 'When God's hand is continually turned against us, we are tempted to think that His head is turned against us too.' So we are. Yet how little we really understand God. It would be far better at such times to sing,

> His love in time past
> Forbids me to think
> He'll leave me at last
> In trouble to sink;
> Each sweet Ebenezer
> I have in review
> Confirms His good pleasure
> To help me quite through.
>
> (John Newton).

It is true that troubles rarely seem to come alone. So often we get the feeling that before we can recover from one calamity we are stricken with another. Yet while the emphasis in verse 3 is on the repeated strokes of the divine hand, 'again and again, all day long', there is a kind heart behind the strong hand – the kind heart of an all-wise, ever-loving, heavenly Father – and not one blow more than is necessary will be permitted to fall. There is a fruitful line of Bible study to follow through here. Let me just point it out. Romans 8:18 and 2 Corinthians 4:17 give us the *perspective* for seeing our afflictions and trials – that of eternity; while James 1:2-4,17 give us the *purpose*, or one of the key purposes, in respect of those experiences – affliction ripens character and is not just bald punishment for punishment's sake. So long as the Lord's hand continues against us we should maintain a prayerful searching of our hearts, and here, yet once more, Psalm 139:23-24 can be such a help.

'He has made my skin and my flesh grow old and has broken my bones,' continues Jeremiah in verse 4. This verse reminds us that illness often makes people look older than they are. We speak of someone 'growing old before his time'. Grief has the same effect sometimes. The skin contracts and wrinkles, while the strength is sapped and exhausted. The verb translated here 'grow old' means to 'wear out by rubbing, to cause to fall away'. It is applied in Scripture to clothes and therefore to bodies (see Job 13:28).

'He has besieged me and surrounded me with bitterness and
hardship' (3:5). The word for 'bitterness' is 'gall', a plant and
its fruit of obscure identification, often associated with
wormwood, very bitter to the taste and used metaphorically
to refer to unpleasant experiences. As such it is suitably
descriptive of the effects of sin – which is precisely the
people's problem over which Jeremiah is agonizing.
The climax of God appearing as an enemy comes in verse 6.
'He has made me dwell in darkness like those long dead.' The
prophet felt that God had involved him in such a depth of distress that he was as incapable of helping or extricating himself
as someone who had been dead for ages would be to escape
from the realms of darkness.

3. God has hemmed him in

The pictures of being besieged and dwelling in darkness
already carry the sense of being shut up, hemmed in, pressed
down, and that is developed now in 3:7-9. The prophet feels
as if he is trapped by a wall around him, or weighed down with
a chain: 'He has walled me in so that I cannot escape; he has
weighed me down with chains' (3:7). The walling up of prison-
ers within confined spaces so that they suffered a fairly speedy
death was a favourite form of torture with the Assyrians.
Even the door of prayer seemed shut, for he testifies, 'Even
when I call out or cry for help, he shuts out my prayer' (3:8).
The verb 'shut out' is 'to stop the prayer', that is, not to prevent prayer from issuing from the heart, nor to restrain actual
supplication, but to prevent the prayer from reaching God's
ear.
And nothing seems straight, or clear, or to be going right
any longer: 'He has barred my way with blocks of stone; he has
made my paths crooked' (3:9). Jeremiah is like a prisoner
whose 'pathway of life' God has barred with insurmountable
obstacles, and whose paths the Lord has made 'crooked'. Literally he says, 'My paths He has turned', that is, 'He has
rendered them such that I cannot walk in them.'
Can you sympathize with his feelings? Do you know anything of this? Does the prophet's honesty strike any chords in

your own heart and experience, as you have trod the pilgrim path?

4. God has left him without help

The burden of the preceding verses has been how the prophet (who represents the people, remember) was deprived of all means of escape from calamity and affliction. Now, in 3:10-15, the emphasis is upon the positive weapons of assault upon him.

In the first place, God is depicted as a wild animal who is ready to tear in pieces whatever crosses its path, **'like a bear lying in wait, like a lion in hiding'** (3:10). It may seem harsh or strange to compare the Lord God to a bear or a lion. But it is not so surprising when we recall that we have already learned from Lamentations that the 'feel' of God's wrath is so terrifying to His people that no words can be found that are really sufficient to express the atrocious nature of their calamities. God had said, 'For I will be like a lion to Ephraim, like a great lion to Judah. I will tear them to pieces and go away; I will carry them off, with no one to rescue them' (Hosea 5:14), and now He has made His word good. The result is set out in verse 11: **'He dragged me from the path and mangled me and left me without help.'** The phrase 'without help' (AV, 'desolate') comes from a root meaning to be motionless, filled with dread, struck with terror, appalled, astonished, stupefied. It seems to be a favourite word with Jeremiah, occurring more than forty times in his prophecy and five times in Lamentations.

The picture (though not the theme) changes in verse 12 to that of God as an unerring marksman or 'a skilled huntsman shooting deadly arrows at his prey'.[3] In 2:4 God 'strung his bow.' Here **'He drew his bow and made me the target for his arrows.'** The arrows are the ills, afflictions and sorrows which God had appointed for His people in consequence of their rebellion and sin. Matthew Henry remarks, 'God has many arrows in His quiver, and they fly swiftly and pierce deeply,' while Lange comments, 'The Lord not only aims at the mark, He hits it and that right in the centre.' Hence verse 13: **'He pierced my heart with arrows from his quiver,'** the point being that God had dealt so severely with His people that no parts (not even, as it were, the innermost parts) were left untouched.

There is probably a connection of thought between verses 13 and 14 as Jeremiah writes. The arrows of verse 13 are no doubt, at least in part, the arrows of derision (3:14), and Jeremiah confesses, **'I became the laughing-stock of all my people; they mock me in song all day long.'** In Jeremiah 9:8 he actually calls a deceitful tongue a deadly arrow. And he knew all too well what it was, in his own experience, to be derided, mocked and made a laughing-stock. However, in his case, as an individual, he was an object of ridicule only to his fellow-citizens, while Jerusalem and Judah have become the laughing-stock of all the nations round about, and, in effect, of the whole world.

This sense of utter helplessness is pressed home even further in verse 15; **'He has filled me with bitter herbs and sated me with gall.'** On this, Calvin has a useful comment: 'The unbelieving nourish their bitterness, for they do not unburden their souls into the bosom of God. But the best way of comfort is when we do not flatter ourselves in our bitterness and grief, but seek the purifying of our souls and in a manner lay them open, so that whatever bitter thing may be there, God may take it away and so feed us ... with the sweetness of His goodness.'

What, honestly, is your response to God if ever your experience comes remotely along the lines of verse 15?

5. God has taken away his hope

Right from the start of the book a sad and gloomy note has been struck, and it has been growing deeper all the time. These verses (3:16-18) are some of the saddest and gloomiest of all.

Look at verse 16: **'He has broken my teeth with gravel; he has trampled me in the dust.'** The sense here seems to combine on the one hand the discomfort and damage to the teeth when food is mingled with the grit of the ashes in which it was cooked, with, on the other, the picture of the prophet actually himself being smothered in ashes. Either way, it is a highly unpleasant and far from nourishing experience. On the first part of verse 16 Calvin comments, 'It is a metaphor taken from those who press stones instead of bread under their teeth; for when grit lies hid in bread, it hurts the teeth. Then inward and hidden griefs are said to be like small stones, which break or shatter the teeth.' The whole verse is a graphic description of acute suffering and shame. And that was precisely the people's lot.

To add to this, Jeremiah speaks in verse 17 of having lost all peace and prosperity: **'I have been deprived of peace; I have forgotten what prosperity is.'** Peace, in Hebrew, indicates all-round health and happiness. In life the Jews greet each other with 'Peace be to you', and in death they have 'in peace' engraved on their sepulchres. But as he reviews his situation (again, personifying in himself the situation of the people in their extremity) he has the feeling that peace is not only out of reach, but out of sight as well. There is no enjoyment in the present and no hope for the future. There is nothing left to live for. He has given up all hopes of attaining safety and prosperity and, all in all, a more desperate, pitiable and forlorn condition is difficult to imagine.

But there is one worse thing still to come. His hope in the Lord is gone too. He underlines this with a **'so I say'** in verse 18: **'My splendour is gone and all that I had hoped from the Lord.'** It is as if he is saying, 'My confidence is no longer directed towards God; indeed it is rather turned right away from Him, so I have lost it altogether. It is completely destroyed. I can no longer stay myself upon God as my support. I cannot any longer hold out any hope for His intervention on my behalf. My whole case seems to be without any possible remedy.'

Everything certainly looks black. And so it is, with good cause. But here in verse 18, for the first time in the chapter, the Lord is actually mentioned by name (Jehovah, the covenant name). This – at the very moment of the deepest note of misery and hopelessness – reminds us of the great truth of Proverbs 18:10 that 'The name of the Lord is a strong tower; the righteous run to it and are safe,' and prepares us for the much-needed brighter prospects that begin to open up at last in the next section.

Before we move on, however, let us be absolutely sure that we have grasped the main line of application to our consciences and hearts. It could not be more contemporary: the appalling condition into which wilful sin brings God's people, whether you think of an individual Christian on his own or the church of God taken together. That is why the language of the chapter, in which God is described as against His people, as an enemy to His people, as hemming His people in, and leaving them without help and taking away their hope, is by no means too strong.

Such a condition will of necessity be characterized by three things.

1. The closing up of the door of prayer

Look again at verse 8, and then meditate upon Psalm 66:18, where the psalmist acknowledges, 'If I had cherished sin in my heart, the Lord would not have listened.' Perhaps this is one of the worst extremities of sin, when you find it of no avail to cry and pray to God. There is nothing in all the world that hinders the believer's praying like hidden, harboured, cherished sin. There are plenty of other reasons for the closing up of the door of prayer, of course, and Benjamin Keach lists a number of them – such as praying in a manner that is not according to God's will, for God's Word must be the rule of our prayers (1 John 5:14); praying when our end or aim is not right (James 4:3); praying in a doubting, unbelieving or faithless frame (James 1:6).[4] All of these things, and others besides, hinder and obstruct the whole business of prayer. But nothing, *nothing,* has this effect so much as sin cherished and unconfessed.

2. The making our paths crooked

Jeremiah said as much in verse 9. 'It is just with God to make those who walk in the crooked paths of sin, crossing God's law, walk in the crooked paths of affliction, crossing their designs.'[5] Putting it more colloquially, we may say that if we walk in the crooked paths of sin we need not be surprised if we end up in the crooked paths of sorrow, from which we shall be powerless, in ourselves, to escape.

> Trust and obey, for there's no other way
> To be happy in Jesus but to trust and obey.
>   (John H. Sammis).

3. The removal of our peace

Jeremiah confessed in verse 17: 'I have been deprived of peace.' The AV has 'And thou hast removed my soul far off from peace.' Peace with God is a given condition to the children of God. 'Therefore, since we have been justified through faith, we have peace with God through our Lord Jesus Christ' (Romans 5:1). But the precious sense of that peace of God will be a variable experience, most grievously affected when we walk in the paths of sin (Philippians 4:7; 1 John 1:5-10). If you 'sin for your profit' you will never 'profit by your sins', but will always end up in trouble.

6.
'The Lord is my portion'

Please read Lamentations 3:19-36

What a different atmosphere suddenly greets us as we continue in chapter 3! It is like one of those days when the heavy clouds begin to disperse and the day clears for a time.

We left the prophet in utter desolation in verse 18, saying, 'My splendour is gone and all that I had hoped from the Lord.' Yet while verses 19-20 still continue the same theme, the prospect becomes altogether different. The four nouns of verse 19, **'affliction ... wandering ... bitterness ... gall'**, continue to express the depths of Jeremiah's sorrow, and the thought behind verses 20-21 is, 'The more I think of my sorrow, the deeper I sink into despair. It is high time I set my eyes upon the Lord.' The thought is, surely, familiar to all of us. Memory, instead of being the servant of despondency, as it so often is, becomes instead the handmaid of hope: **'I remember ... I well remember ... yet this I call to mind.'** Herein is the change: the prophet's mind and heart settle afresh upon the glorious divine attributes of God in their unchanging and unchangeable beauty. When sin drives the soul from God, its hope perishes. Only as the soul returns to God is its hope restored.

In a sermon on 3:21, C. H. Spurgeon uses this illustration: 'At the south of Africa the sea was generally so stormy when the frail barks of the Portuguese went sailing south that they named it the Cape of Storms; but after that cape had been well rounded by bolder navigators, they named it the Cape of Good Hope. In your experience you had many a Cape of Storms, but you have weathered them all, and now let them be a Cape of Good Hope to you.'

Having observed, then, from verses 19-21 the connection
with what has gone before, we can divide the new section
helpfully into three parts:

God's great faithfulness	3:22-26
Man's great benefit	3:27-30
Three great principles about God	3:31-36

God's great faithfulness

The familiar statement **'Great is your faithfulness'** (3:23) is
demonstrated here in four different ways.

1. God's faithfulness in the midst of the greatest afflictions

From verse 22 Jeremiah drops the first person singular for a
while as he speaks. The testimony here begins: **'Because of the
Lord's great love we are not consumed.'** For 'great love', the
AV has 'mercies', which captures the fact that the word is in
the plural, denoting the abundance and variety of these mercies. The word refers to the covenant loyalties or covenant
mercies of God towards His people. It is a grand word – incor-
porating His loving-kindness, grace, favour and goodness.
And those mercies are the *only* reason why we are not 'consumed', overwhelmed, destroyed, by the dangers of life and
the follies we bring upon ourselves on account of our sin.
Psalm 103:10 comes immediately to mind: 'He does not treat
us as our sins deserve or repay us according to our iniquities.'
And the verse continues, **'For his compassions never fail.'**
God's 'compassions' are His pity, sympathetic love and kindness, especially to the needy, helpless and destitute. They
never fail. This stream runs on and on, but never runs dry.
Why? Because these are the compassions of the changeless
and eternal God!
Listen to Matthew Henry as he applies this to God's
people, the church: 'The church of God is like Moses' bush,
burning, yet not consumed; whatever hardships it has met
with, or may meet with, it shall have a being in the world to
the end of time. It is persecuted of men, but not forsaken of
God, and therefore though it is cast down, it is not destroyed;
corrected, yet not consumed; refined in the furnace as silver,

but not consumed as dross.' Remember that God never leaves Himself without a remnant and a witness even in the worst of days and the darkest hour. By the grace of God, His people (whether in Jeremiah's day or our own) are not utterly ruined or destroyed. God's compassions never fail, even when He *appears* to have shut them up.

2. God's faithfulness in the daily renewal of divine mercies

The first word of verse 23, **'they'**, refers back, of course, to God's mercies and compassions just mentioned. Every morning ushers in new evidences of these precious things. Just picture the dreary situation at the time when these words were spoken (and 1:1-3:18 has left us in no doubt as to its nature!). 'Every breath, every sip of water, every crust of bread, every stitch of clothing is regarded by the prophet as evidence of the ever new inexhaustible mercies and compassions of the Lord.'[1]

The description that they are **'new every morning'** is as beautiful and true as it is poetic and evocative. I came across this lovely comment upon it: 'Every divine blessing has the freshness and fragrance of the morning about it – unfailing as the morning dawn, bright and joyous as the morning sunshine, brilliant and sparkling as the morning dew, sweet and invigorating as the morning air.'[2] It is no wonder that the hymn-writer Thomas Chisholm was moved to write:

> Great is Thy faithfulness! Great is Thy faithfulness!
> Morning by morning new mercies I see;
> All I have needed Thy hand hath provided –
> Great is Thy faithfulness, Lord, unto me!

And in his final verse he names some of these mercies:

> Pardon for sin and a peace that endureth,
> Thy own dear presence to cheer and to guide;
> Strength for today and bright hope for tomorrow,
> Blessings all mine, with ten thousand beside!

There is nothing stale about God's mercies and compassions. Our needs are constant, and so is the divine provision. Daily mercies are continual reminders of divine faithfulness.

3. God's faithfulness in giving an assured foundation to our soul's hope

Verse 24 is without doubt one of the loveliest verses in Lamentations, and surely in the whole of the Bible. The description of the Lord as the believer's and the church's **'portion'** is not exclusive to this verse, though. Particularly memorable is Psalm 73:25-26: 'Whom have I in heaven but you? And earth has nothing I desire besides you. My flesh and my heart may fail, but God is the strength of my heart and my portion for ever.' That quotation goes a long way to capturing the whole sense of the word 'portion'. God is 'the all-sufficient happiness of His people', says Matthew Henry (cf. Psalm 16:5-6; 119:57). The expression is probably based on Numbers 18:20, where 'The Lord said to Aaron, "You will have no inheritance in their land, nor will you have any share among them; I am your share and your inheritance among the Israelites."' In other words, the Lord God Jehovah would be to the tribe of Levi what the other tribes received in their territorial possessions in Canaan. Levi did not have such possessions; that tribe's whole possession and enjoyment was to be in the Lord Himself.

'Portion' comes from a root meaning 'to divide'. 'The Lord is my part, my lot, and with this portion I rest fully satisfied.' Speaking in such a spirit, Jeremiah is an example to the people that they too should seek their comfort in the Lord alone – not least, because we know that all other, earthly, portions perish and fail, whereas the Lord is our portion for ever. There is a moving testimony to the truth of this in Andrew Bonar's diary. His wife, Isabella, died on 14 October 1864. Writing in his diary on the anniversary of her death more than twenty years later (1887) he noted: 'Memorable to me as the anniversary of my beloved Isabella's sudden departure to be with Christ. And now my son's son, a child of three days old, has been taken from them. Broken cisterns, broken cisterns all around: but the fountain remains full.'[3] Only those who are satisfied with God alone will not be seized with impatience, folly and anxiety when troubles come. We have His great salvation, continual presence, unerring wisdom, fatherly care, infallible guidance, everlasting love, eternal inheritance, complete sufficiency and, most of all, we have Him!

There is a very rich treatment of this theme, 'The Lord is my portion', in volume 2 of the works of Thomas Brooks. In a brief appendix to this commentary I have sought to summarize one or two of its gems. Here is a taste for now: 'A man that has God for his portion is the rarest and happiest man in the world; he is like the morning star in the midst of the clouds; he is like the moon when it is at full; he is like the flower of the roses in the spring of the year; he is like the lilies by the springs of waters; he is like the branches of frankincense in the time of summer; he is like a vessel of gold that is set about with all manner of precious stones.' The point is this, you see: with God as his portion, what more could any man want? Notice Jeremiah's remark, **'I say to myself.'** Here is a great line of self-encouragement – with the very desirable practical effect of rest, contentment and patience in Him. For it is in direct relation to the fact that 'The Lord is my portion' that Jeremiah says, **'Therefore I will wait for him.'**

Referring all this to our Jehovah Jesus, whom the Father has made to us 'all, and ... in all' (Colossians 3:11), Charles Wesley writes:

Thou hidden source of calm repose,
    Thou all-sufficient love divine;
My help and refuge from my foes,
    Secure I am, if Thou art mine:
From sin and grief, from guilt and shame,
I hide me, Jesus, in Thy name.

Thy mighty name salvation is
    And keeps my happy soul above;
Comfort it brings, and power and peace
    And joy and everlasting love:
To me, with Thy dear name, are given
Pardon and holiness and heaven.

Jesus, my all in all Thou art,
  My rest in toil, mine ease in pain;
The medicine of my broken heart;
  In war, my peace; in loss, my gain;
My smile beneath the tyrant's frown;
In shame, my glory and my crown.

In want, my plentiful supply;
  In weakness, mine almighty power;
In bonds, my perfect liberty;
  My light in Satan's darkest hour;
My help and stay whene'er I call;
My life in death; my heaven, my all.

4. God's faithfulness in His proven goodness to His waiting people

For a start, verse 25 is a confirmation of verse 24. The Lord's being our portion speaks to us of His sheer goodness. 'The Lord is good to all' (Psalm 145:9), but especially, our text affirms, is He **'good to those whose hope is in him'** – good to His own. And a mark of 'those whose hope is in Him' is that they seek Him (3:25) and **'wait quietly for the salvation of the Lord'** (3:26). The word 'salvation' here means His deliverance or coming to their aid.

What is it, in the context, to seek Him? Surely it is to acknowledge how greatly and continually we need His mercy, to go directly to Him when temptation assaults us and to flee to Him for aid in the face of every trouble and danger. Matthew Henry remarks, 'It is good (our duty, and will be our unspeakable comfort and satisfaction) to hope ... and wait ... though the difficulties that lie in the way of it seem insupportable ... though it be long delayed; and while we wait to be quiet and silent, not quarrelling with God nor making ourselves weary, but aquiescing in the divine disposals.' And George Barlow makes the further important practical point: 'Murmuring begets murmuring, and we are apt to blame everyone but ourselves. The more we grumble, the farther are we away from goodness. It is only when we are silent and abstain from complaining that we begin to see that our deliverance must come from God.' Hope in God, the apostle Paul reminds us, 'does not disappoint us, because God has poured out his love into our hearts by the Holy Spirit, whom he has given us' (Romans 5:5).

Here, then, in verses 22-26, are some approved texts and rich cordials for all the stricken hearts of God's people. Learn them by heart. Meditate upon them and all they assure us of: the goodness of the Lord, the great love of the Lord, the unfailing compassions of the Lord, the faithfulness of the Lord. These are the comforts of God's people in an evil day. Behold here 'the encouragement of the Scriptures' (Romans 15:4), not least in those days when our hearts are discouraged or full of fears and objections. Let us cultivate for ourselves and towards one another that lovely ministry of Jonathan to David who, when David was on the run from Saul and under great pressure from enemies on every side, went to him, met with him and 'helped him to find strength in God' ('strengthened his hand in God', AV, 1 Samuel 23:16).

Man's great benefit

The message of verses 27-30 is simple, though more easily said than learned: afflictions are good for us! Moreover, says Jeremiah, **'It is good for a man to bear the yoke while he is young'** (3:27). Calvin wonders whether the yoke of instruction, or teaching, is intended rather than the yoke of chastisement, or scourges. While you can trace the teaching and the discipline harnessed together in, say, Ephesians 6:4, it is generally agreed, and certainly suits the context, to take it here as the yoke of God's afflictions. It is *His* yoke that we are to bear, and it will add greatly to our support under and profit from our afflictions to see and acknowledge His sovereign hand and power upon us.

Why especially in the days of youth? There are various reasons. One is that youth is proverbially a time of freshness, vigour and strength, all of which speak of a greater ability to bear the yoke. But there is a more important set of reasons. It develops humility and seriousness at an early age, when there can be a great natural tendency to flippancy and lightheartedness. It weans the young believer from the world and teaches him from the start to set his affections on things above – even upon Christ Himself, in whom our life is hid. It is greatly glorifying to God to see young people living for eternity, and gripped by the assurance that 'Our light and momentary troubles are achieving for us an eternal glory that far outweighs them all. So we fix our eyes not on what is seen, but on what is unseen. For what is seen is temporary, but what is unseen is eternal' (2 Corinthians 4:17-18). Youth is that time when people are most susceptible to instruction and when there is the greatest danger of being corrupted (cf. 2 Timothy 2:22); it is the time when temptations to sin may be strongest.

And it renders the bearing of burdens easier in later life. The one who has known what it is to bear the yoke while he is young should be less likely to sink into despair and unbelief or to collapse under the weight of the yoke in later years. That is why the psalmist could testify, 'It was good for me to be afflicted,' in order that 'I might learn your decrees' (Psalm 119:71). His was not some super-spirituality or false piety, but the genuine testimony of one who had not only been brought to know the Lord while he was young but had also learned to bear the Lord's yoke while he was young.

Matthew Henry contributes an important observation from the historical context of Lamentations. Many of the young men had been carried off into captivity in exile. We have noticed a number of times the sad refrain concerning the death or exile of the young men and women. 'To make them easy in it, Jeremiah tells them that it was good for them to bear the yoke of the captivity, and they would find it so if they would but accommodate themselves to their condition and labour to answer God's ends in laying that heavy yoke upon them.' And it is worth noting that Jeremiah himself bore the yoke in his youth. According to Jeremiah 1:6 he was young when God called him to be a prophet, and from the very beginning he experienced much opposition and many trials. Having himself learned to bear the yoke early in life, he was the better able to do so later in life, and to encourage others as they, too, had to bear it.

Though the least mention in Scripture of the yoke will make us think of the Saviour's words in Matthew 11:28, there is no direct tie-up between our verse, which refers to the yoke of affliction, and the verse in Matthew, which speaks of the yoke of God's commands and discipleship – except for one very important particular. It is never too early – you can never be too young – to come under Christ's yoke, the gospel yoke, of repentance, faith and obedience. To become a Christian while you are still young is a most blessed thing. It brings you gospel comforts sooner. It keeps you from endless snares, which you would be in danger of falling into in pursuing an ungodly life. And it gives you, if the Lord spares you, a longer time in which to serve God on earth, prior to reigning with Him in heaven.

The remainder of this section indicates the manner in which this yoke is to be borne to God's glory and our benefit: in godly fear (3:28), with reverent humility (3:29) and without resentment (3:30).

1. Godly fear

The picture in verse 28 is of sedateness and quietness before God. **'Let him sit alone in silence, for the Lord has laid it on him.'** Laetsch comments, 'Let him learn to suffer in silence and not to murmur against the Lord who has sent the tribulation.'

2. Reverent humility

Verse 29 depicts an attitude of humility and patience before God. **'Let him bury his face in the dust,'** is a token of entire submission to the Lord, humbly bowing beneath His mighty hand. Evidently the expression comes from the Oriental custom of throwing oneself in the most reverential manner on the ground, with the mouth placed in the dust so that it cannot speak. There is no abandoning of self to complaints, no moaning about injuries done, and no asking, 'What have I done to deserve this?' Yet while we are to show this sort of resignation, it is *hopeful,* not *hopeless.* **'There may yet be hope'** that God will bring deliverance from all our troubles.

3. No resentment

The attitude portrayed in verse 30 is one of meekness and mildness towards those who may be the instruments of our troubles and a willingness to show a forgiving spirit: **'Let him**

offer his cheek to one who would strike him, and let him be filled with disgrace.' The call to offer your cheek (cf. Matthew 5:38-39) was exemplified supremely by the Lord Jesus Christ Himself (Matthew 26:67; John 18:22; 19:3; Isaiah 50:6). Is this how, with the Lord's help, we react in times of affliction and trial?

There is a certain gradation in the three verses here that is hard to miss: the sitting alone in silence is one thing, difficult enough, but maybe easier than placing your mouth in the dust while still clinging to hope; but then comes the most difficult of all – giving your cheek to the smiter and submitting to personal disgrace and dishonour.

> Oh, for a faith that will not shrink,
> Though pressed by many a foe;
> That will not tremble on the brink
> Of poverty or woe;
>
> That will not murmur or complain
> Beneath the chastening rod;
> But in the hour of grief and pain
> Can lean upon its God!

> (William H Bathurst).

Three great principles about God

These are each intended to motivate the attitudes under trial that have just been described.

God will not cast off His people for ever

Remember that the Lord is the One whose 'compassions never fail'. His mercy to His people is not only 'new every morning' but is everlasting. So whether His yoke upon us is a direct chastisement or rather a trial in a different context without the element of punishment, we may be sure that, according to the terms of His gracious covenant with His people, **'Men are not cast off by the Lord for ever'** (3:31). 'We may bear ourselves up with this,' remarks Matthew Henry, 'that when we are cast down, yet we are not cast off.' And he adds, 'The father's correcting his son is not a disinheriting of him.'

Look at the richness of verse 32: **'Though he brings grief, he will show compassion, so great is his unfailing love.'** All our sorrows will come to an end. And notice this: the very God who 'brings grief' is the One who 'will show compassion', and that not according to what we deserve, which is in fact nothing, but according to His endless mercies! See here the fulness of God's grace. Take a close look at Isaiah 54:7-8 and Psalm 89:30-34. Whenever God's visitations have achieved their end, He is pleased to remove His afflicting hand. And He always knows exactly how much of that hand we need and how much of it we can bear (cf. 1 Corinthians 10:13).

God will never afflict us 'willingly'

What is meant by that word **'willingly'** in verse 33? 'For he does not willingly bring affliction or grief to the children of men.' It is, in fact, one of the most encouraging verses in the Bible. The word is literally 'from the heart', and what it means is that God does not afflict us for pleasure or excitement, for no reason, or for something to do. It is only when we provoke Him to jealousy, or in some other way give Him just cause, and even then (as verse 32 has just declared) He will in due time bring us fresh seasons of His compassion and unfailing love. God delights neither in the death of sinners nor the disquiet of saints. There is, if it is proper to put it this way, a certain reluctance in God when it comes to the matter of His people's afflictions. We are not, as cynics, unbelievers and the devil himself would have it, balls that God enjoys bouncing and kicking around. He does not love to make a spectacle of us or in any way gloat over us in our afflictions. '[His people] may by faith see love in His heart even when they see frowns in His face and a rod in His hand.'[4]

All this because He tells us Himself that He does not afflict us 'willingly'! How do we know? We know from his character: He is our God of covenant love. We know from that relationship He sustains to His people: He is not just their Maker, but their Redeemer, Father and Husband. We know from the fact that our sufferings are accompanied with many alleviations;

if He took pleasure in dealing heavily with us, surely He
would not mingle so much mercy with His judgements.
And we know from the object He has in view for us when he
afflicts His children: not our temporary, fleeting happiness
but our eternal, lasting holiness.

God is the God of justice

As the Lord Himself is not a cruel taskmaster, so wrongs committed by men do not meet with His approval. That is the
message of the closing verses of this section (3:34-36), which
form one connected sentence. The same principle applies,
whether it be the cruel treatment of the Jews by the Babylonians at the taking of Jerusalem, or deeds of violence perpet-
rated generally by victors in war, **'to crush underfoot all pris-
oners in the land'** (3:34); or the crimes of offences against the
proper administration of justice, denials of human rights, **'to
deny a man his rights before the Most High'** (3:35); or unjust
practices in the carrying on of ordinary everyday life, **'to
deprive a man of justice'** (3:36). Of all such practices the
prophet asks, **'Would not the Lord see such things?'** Indeed
He does see them, and He abhors them. No act of wrongdo-
ing, whether committed in secret or out in the open, can
escape Jehovah's all-seeing eye – nor can it escape His
punishment.

And another thing. Although (as in the present context
concerning Babylon) God sometimes makes use of men as
instruments in His hand to correct His people, yet He is still
very far from being pleased with any outrages or injustices
which those instruments might commit against them. He does
not turn a blind eye to the goings-on in the world. He does not
overlook all the blasphemies against His own name. He does
not remain indifferent to the injustice of man to man. He does
not fail to keep an account of all the wrongs done to His
people. And sooner or later He will require a reckoning.

7.
Man before God

Please read Lamentations 3:37-54

As this lengthy central chapter of Lamentations continues, there is no let-up in the passionate and emotional feeling and expression of the prophet Jeremiah on behalf of the people. This new section divides usefully into three portions, and is rich in spiritual instruction.

God's rule

Drawing his teaching from his experience of the sins of the covenant people of God and His judgements on them to correct and restore them, Jeremiah now dwells upon the absolute and universal nature of God's rule. Every Christian and, for that matter, every human being, needs to know of God's sovereign rule, power and dominion. And for the believer this doctrine is no mere lip-service but is gloriously true and thoroughly practical. It is the song of the redeemed both on earth and in heaven:

'To him who sits on the throne and to the Lamb
be praise and honour and glory and power,
    for ever and ever!'
                                    (Revelation 5:13).

Verses 37-39 are tremendously helpful in answering the question: 'How does God's sovereignty apply to the Christian?' We can discern three principles to lean upon.

1. Nothing happens without God's knowledge and sanction

'**Who can speak and have it happen if the Lord has not decreed
it?**' (3:37). Start with the historical circumstances. The
Babylonians had said they would destroy Jerusalem, and that
is exactly what they had done. But why did it happen? Was it
because they had said they would do it? The answer is, it happened because God, the sovereign God, commanded and
commissioned them to do it. What are men but tools which
the great God takes up and puts down, uses and finishes with,
as He pleases in the government of the world? God is not
some idle or forgetful deity, sitting back comfortably in
heaven, leading an inactive life, giving up the world to
chance, letting things happen, or even doing things Himself at
random. The repeated truth of the Bible is that 'The Lord
reigns!'

> The Lord is King! Lift up your voice,
> O earth, and all ye heavens, rejoice!
> From world to world the joy shall ring,
> The Lord omnipotent is King!
>
> (Josiah Conder).

Calvin remarks that God decreed before the world was
made whatever He was to do, and so there is nothing now
done in the world which is not directed by His counsel. As it
was in creation, of which we read, 'For he spoke, and it came
to be; he commanded, and it stood firm' (Psalm 33:9), so it is
in administration or government: 'Our God is in heaven ; he
does whatever pleases him' (Psalm 115:3). None of this, let it
be added hastily, makes God the author or originator of sin
and evil. Yet He does turn the wrath of man to His own
praise, and causes grace to abound where sin has previously
abounded.

All of this is tremendously important and encouraging.
What seem so often to us to be chances, accidents, freaks,
catastrophes or mistakes all fit in with the action of God's
decrees and His governing will. (See Proverbs 16:9, Isaiah
43:13; 46:10.) And it all comes home to the believer's heart in
the form of that richest of divine cordials: 'And we know that
in all things God works for the good of those who love him,

who have been called according to his purpose' (Romans 8:28).

2. *It is God Himself who orders all things*

'Is it not from the mouth of the Most High that both calamities and good things come?' (3:38). This is not just a repetition of the first principle. It goes further or, better, it becomes more personal and particular. It is the easiest thing in the world for God's people to acknowledge God's sovereignty and goodness when everything is going well and we are sailing on a silver sea, even though (we say it to our shame) we are often slow and neglectful in doing so. But verse 38 states confidently that not only 'good things' but 'calamities' also come 'from the mouth [i.e., the decree] of the Most High'. Whatever we receive – health or sickness, smooth waters or rough seas, wealth or poverty, success or disappointment, loneliness or friendship, even life or death – is from God, the Most High God, and determined by Him in the light of His wise and gracious providences.

It was a saying among some older writers that 'God is too wise to err, too good to be unkind.' Job grasped this. Remember how, when his wife had been trying to get him to 'curse God and die!', he said to her, 'You are talking like a foolish woman. Shall we accept good from God, and not trouble?' (Job 2:10). John Flavel penned his famous (and highly recommended) treatise *The Mystery of Providence* on the text Psalm 57:2, which in the AV reads, 'God that performeth all things for me', and in the NIV, 'God who fulfils his purpose for me.'[1] This is the child of God's blessed assurance!

3. *We must never quarrel with God*

'Why should any living man complain when punished for his sins?' (3:39). Think of it this way. Unbelievers are very quick to turn on God in their troubles (the God in whom they do not 'believe' the rest of the time!) and murmur against Him and hold Him responsible. And believers are also sometimes all too quick to do something very similar. But it is so wrong, and so sinful. If a man brings sickness upon himself by deliberately taking a wrong or poisonous medicine, what reason has he to blame the medicine? After all, he took it! And so what grounds of complaint against God has any living person because of the evils and miseries that he has brought upon himself by his own deliberate sins? The inhabitants of Judah and Jerusalem needed to remember this.

Matthew Henry remarks, 'Though we may pour out our complaints before God, we must never exhibit any complaints against God.' Whenever we are tempted to quarrel with God we need to keep alive in our hearts a fresher and deeper sense of God's love towards us, not one drop of which did we ever deserve! Think again of Job. 'The Lord said to Job: "Will the one who contends with the Almighty correct him? Let him who accuses God answer him!"' (Job 40:1-2). Now have a look at the response which that drew from Job in verses 3-5 of the same chapter! Maybe here in our passage in Lamentations, Jeremiah is checking himself in some way for some of his own earlier complaints. Whatever God does, we must never open our mouths against Him. Positively, the apostle Paul puts it this way: 'Godliness with contentment is great gain' (1 Timothy 6:6). Do we demonstrate this?

A remarkable illustration of this is to be found in the life of General Stonewall Jackson. He was once asked, 'Suppose, in addition to blindness, you were condemned to be bedridden and racked with pain for life; you would hardly call yourself happy then?' He paused, and said with great deliberateness, 'Yes, I think I could. My faith in the almighty wisdom is absolute, and why should this accident change it?' In order to press him further, the question was then put: 'If, in addition to blindness and incurable infirmity and pain, you had to receive grudging charity from those on whom you had no claim, what then?' The questioner knew he was touching Jackson here on a tender point – his impatience of anything bordering on dependence. We are told that there was a strange reverence in the general's lifted eye, and an exalted expression over his whole face, as he replied with slow deliberateness, 'If it was God's will, I think I could lie there content a hundred years!'

A. W. Pink, in his classic little book on the sovereignty of God, has a chapter entitled 'Our attitude towards God's sovereignty'.[2] What should our attitude be? One, he says, of godly fear, implicit obedience, entire resignation, deep thankfulness and joy and of adoring worship. Have we not still got a lot to learn?

A call to repentance

Jeremiah has not been reminding the people of God's sovereign rule purely for doctrinal reasons. He desires the doctrine to have a dynamic effect in their lives. And so this next section (3:40-42) arises very naturally out of the set of three questions we have just considered in verses 37-39.

We have seen that when God punishes sin justly, no sinner has any reason to complain, and that when God punishes the sins of His people, His children, then we have no cause for complaint. Indeed, if He did not punish sin He would be inconsistent with Himself as the all-holy God, and that is something He can never be! And the dynamic effect in the people's lives needs to be repentance, but the real thing, not a phoney or a counterfeit. Remember Joel 2:13: 'Rend your heart and not your garments. Return to the Lord your God, for he is gracious and compassionate, slow to anger and abounding in love, and he relents from sending calamity.' Harrison remarks, 'The appeal for spiritual renewal is concerned with internal motivation, not the kind of external ritual performances of which there had been a surfeit in pre-exilic days.'

Repentance is defined by Thomas Watson as 'a grace of God's Spirit, whereby a sinner is inwardly humbled and visibly reformed'.[3] He then develops that definition by stating that 'Repentance is a spiritual medicine made up of six special ingredients,' and that 'If any one is left out it loses its virtue.' Those six special ingredients he defines as sight of sin, sorrow for sin, confession of sin, shame for sin, hatred for sin and turning from sin. And, for our purposes, the point is this: those same things which should mark the repentance of the sinner who is coming to God through the Lord Jesus Christ in the first place should also be the marks in our lives as believers whenever, having sinned against the Lord, we need to return to Him in repentance for forgiveness. It is possible to trace Watson's six ingredients in our present verses. For this exposition, however, let me group the material under four features.

1. Self-examination

Two verbs are used in the opening statement of verse 40: **'Let us examine our ways and test them.'** The verbs are 'examine' and 'test'. Laetsch informs us that the first means, literally, 'to dig into', to look for what is hidden from our eyes by our deceptive hearts, while the second means to explore so as to become thoroughly acquainted with the object (the word is used in Judges 18:2 and 2 Samuel 10:3 of exploring a city or country). We each have a natural reluctance to attend to this duty, but the fact of the matter is that many of our sins are not easily discovered or acknowledged unless and until such a diligent search is made. We need the aid of the Holy Spirit of God, for we never have any real idea of just how sinful we still are unless, in His powerful exposing light, we undertake this thorough and resolute investigation of our hearts and lives. It has to be said that this is one of the great absent notes in contemporary evangelism; our forefathers in the faith knew so much more about this than we do – which explains why they were the people they were and why we are the people we are.

2. Renewed turning to God

This follows in the same verse, verse 40. **'Let us examine ... and test'** leads straight into **'Let us return to the Lord.'** They are linked by that vital little word 'and': let us do one thing *and* then the other. Here is the difference between a real repentance and a worldly one (cf. 2 Corinthians 7:10). The Hebrew preposition 'to' carries the sense of 'as far as' or 'even to'. Laetsch is again helpful in observing that it includes aiming at your goal and actually arriving there, not stopping short (even nine-tenths of the way).

3. Earnest prayer

The accompaniment of all this must be *earnest prayer.*

Jeremiah speaks in verse 41 of lifting up **'our hearts and our hands to God in heaven'** – an expressive picture of the earnestness and single-mindedness that is involved. We are reminded of Isaiah 29:13: 'The Lord says: "These people come near to me with their mouth and honour me with their lips, but their hearts are far from me."' How useless it is to pray with the mouth only, when the heart is not going along with the words!

Back in verse 38 God was described as 'the Most High'; now in verse 41 He is 'God in heaven' – all to remind us that we must look *up* to Him, 'the One enthroned in heaven' (Psalm 2:4), the One 'seated on a throne' (Isaiah 6:1), in the longing that He would look *down* in mercy and forgiveness upon us.

> 'If you, O Lord, kept a record of sins,
>   O Lord, who could stand?
> But with you there is forgiveness;
>   therefore you are feared'
>
> (Psalm 130:3-4).

4. Confession of sin

With the self-examination, the renewed turning to God and the earnest prayer there is, of necessity, one more thing, and that is confession of sin. The **'and say'** at the end of verse 41 leads into **'We have sinned and rebelled'** (3:42). Both verbs are in the perfect tense, describing the life of the nation as an uninterrupted obstinate rebellion. But we have no stones to throw, for how is it with you and me as the people of God? Surely this has to be our testimony again and again: 'For what I want to do I do not do, but what I hate I do' (Romans 7:15 – cf. 7:19).

And our confession of sin before God needs not only to be general ('I/we have sinned') but to be particularized ('I have sinned *in this*/we have sinned *in that*'), as well as to be accompanied by a pleading and resolution not to commit the same sins again. Thomas Watson remarks that 'Some run from the confessing of sin to the committing of sin.' We need to have the love of sinning taken away from us. But when we have sinned, and have come in confession and repentance, then we

are truly thankful for the gospel glories of 1 John 1:8-2:2, and
for the precious reality of that fountain opened to cleanse us
from sin and impurity – even the blood of the Lord Jesus
Christ, our Saviour (Zechariah 13:1).
But what of the last part of verse 42, **'and you have not for-
given'**? The reason cannot be because God is no longer merciful. It cannot be that He is unwilling to forgive or because the
opportunity is inappropriate in some way. Surely it is to
remind us again of the danger of a lack of reality and sincerity
in repentance. 'God does not mock the sinner by urging to
repentance and then withholding forgiveness. If there is no
eagerness for forgiveness, it is because there is something rad-
ically defective in the repentance.'[4] Is that a word to our own
hearts, or to the hearts of God's church in these days?

'Until the Lord ...'

How frail we are, and how our best intentions fail to
materialize! The prophet has just chided himself and the
people for complaining against God – yet verses 43-54 savour
of that very mistake, as if with a sense of the wounds of God's
judgements being freshly opened and the memory of them
being impossible to erase.
  Let us take a brief general view of the section first of all, and
then comment separately on certain particular matters of
interpretation and application. In a sense it is the same old
story that we have had before in Lamentations, by way of the
consequences of the people's sin. God seems to have withdrawn from His people (3:43-44), the nations have triumphed
over them and brought them to a feeling of utter despair
(3:45-47), which produces tears of anguish and deep grief of
soul (3:48-51) along with the sense of being completely overwhelmed, like a hunted bird, an imprisoned fugitive or a
drowning man (3:52-54). Such is the general lay-out. But
notice some of the details.
  In verses 43-44 we have a terrible picture of God's discipli-
nary dealings with His people. God has 'enveloped Himself in
a cloud of wrath out of which His thunderbolts flash forth
against the rebels in the form of pitiless pursuit and slaying
(v.43), and through which no prayer can penetrate (v.44);

neither the prayers of the people (Jeremiah 14:12) nor of His prophet (Jeremiah 7:16;11:14;14:11;15:1)'.[5] Yet we need not be surprised at the vigour of the language. As Calvin says, 'It is a simple acknowledgement of God's righteous vengeance ... Had they said that they had been leniently chastised, it would have been very strange, for the temple had been burnt, the city had been demolished, the kingdom had been overthrown, the people for the most part had been driven into exile, the remainder had been scattered, the covenant of God had been in a manner abolished.' Moreover, the phrase at the end of verse 44, **'so that no prayer can get through'**, confirms our earlier remark concerning the lack of reality and sincerity in the people's repentance. As we observed in connection with 3:8, the Lord will not listen to us when we continue to cherish sin in our hearts (Psalm 66:18).

'You have made us scum and refuse among the nations' (3:45). The word for 'scum' (AV 'offscouring,) has the sense of 'sweepings' or 'scrapings' and is the only occurrence of the word in the Hebrew Bible. It denotes, says Harrison, 'anything rejected as unfit for use'. It has an equally rare New Testament counterpart in 1 Corinthians 4:13, where Paul says that the apostles 'have become the scum of the earth, the refuse of the world'.

'Terror and pitfalls' (3:47) is literally 'terror and the pit' (that is, destruction), while 'destroyed' at the end of verse 48 links up with a Hebrew verb meaning 'to shelter, wreck, tear in pieces', and so implies what Harrison calls 'the complete termination of organized life in the kingdom'. What an awful picture of absolute breakdown amongst – of all people – the people of God!

In verses 49-51 we see more evidence of Jeremiah as the sorrowing or weeping prophet (cf. Jeremiah 9:1), because of all that has happened and is happening to his people, who are God's people. His testimony, **'What I see brings grief to my soul'** (3:51) is literally, 'My eye does evil to my soul' or 'causes pain to my soul'. His eyes, in other words, have become greatly irritated and weakened because of his much weeping, and this pain in the eye has heightened the agony of his soul. Does Jeremiah's attitude seem strange to us? Or do we know something ourselves of that giving ourselves no rest and giving God no rest 'till he establishes Jerusalem and makes her

the praise of the earth'? (Isaiah 62:7). Have we ever wept for
Zion?

I love Thy kingdom, Lord,
The house of thine abode,
The church our blest Redeemer saved
With His own precious blood.

I love Thy church, O God:
Her walls before Thee stand,
Dear as the apple of Thine eye,
And graven on Thy hand.

For her my tears shall fall,
For her my prayer ascend,
To her my cares and toils be given,
Till toils and cares shall end.

(Timothy Dwight).

There is a major division of opinion among interpreters
over whether the key reference in verses 52-54 is to
Jeremiah's own sufferings (e.g. Jeremiah 38:6) or whether he
is continuing to undertake the cause of the whole people, with
the object of encouraging the faithful, by his own example, to
lament their pitiful state so that they might all obtain pardon
from God. I incline to the latter position. There seems to be
a strong figurative element in the pictures he uses, rather than
the account of one man's actual afflictions and trials. Com-
menting on verse 54, **'The waters closed over my head, and I
thought I was about to be cut off'** ,Matthew Henry remarks,
'The distresses of God's people sometimes prevail to such a
degree that they cannot find any footing for their faith, nor
keep their head above water.'

It all adds up to a picture of unrelieved gloom and misery
still. But wait a moment! Not so fast! There is a ray of light in
verse 50: **'until the Lord looks down from heaven and sees'**.
Compare this with two other choice verses: 'Restore us, O
Lord God Almighty; make your face shine upon us, that we
may be saved' (Psalm 80:19). 'Now, our God, hear the
prayers and petitions of your servant. For your sake, O Lord,
look with favour on your desolate sanctuary' (Daniel 9:17; cf.

vv. 18-19). 'Bad as the case is, one favourable look from heaven will set all to rights.'[6] The hope and longing are expressed that God will yet intervene and come to His people's aid. He will forgive their sins. He will restore them to fellowship with Himself again. He will wipe their tears away. He will comfort them again.

As we consider the desperate condition of the church and people of God in our own day, let us remember this: this God is our God! 'Sing to the Lord, you saints of his; praise his holy name. For his anger lasts only a moment, but his favour lasts a lifetime; weeping may remain for a night, but rejoicing comes in the morning' (Psalm 30:4-5).

8.
Encouraged in God

Please read Lamentations 3:55-66

The heart of true biblical Christianity, true biblical religion, is to know the Lord and, knowing Him, to go on to know Him better and better and better. The Lord Jesus Christ gives this definition of eternal life in John 17:3: 'Now this is eternal life: that they may know you, the only true God, and Jesus Christ, whom you have sent.' And the apostle Peter gives this exhortation: 'But grow in the grace and knowledge of our Lord and Saviour Jesus Christ' (2 Peter 3:18). Yet how much do we really know about the Lord? Or, more to the point and more biblically, how well do we really know the Lord? Jeremiah, the author of Lamentations, records in his prophecy what alone is worth boasting about:

'This is what the Lord says:
"Let not the wise man boast of his wisdom
   or the strong man boast of his strength
   or the rich man boast of his riches,
but let him who boasts boast about this:
   that he understands and knows me,
that I am the Lord ..."'

(Jeremiah 9:23-24).

Is that your boast? And however well you know the Lord already, is it your single-minded goal to press on still further to know Him? The apostle Paul had been on the pilgrim path for a long time when he expressed the deep longing: 'I want to know Christ' (Philippians 3:10).

The section of Lamentations to which we have now come is concerned with this very thing – the believer's and the church's knowledge of God. And it is concerned with this knowledge not from the point of view of pure academic, intellectual interest, but from the practical standpoint of putting it to use in our experience and finding real encouragement in God.

Matthew Henry begins his remarks upon this section by saying, 'We may observe throughout this chapter a struggle in the prophet's breast between sense and faith, fear and hope; he complains and then comforts himself, yet drops his comforts and returns again to his complaints ... but ... faith gets the last word and comes off a conqueror, for in these verses he concludes with some comfort.'

What are some of the chief grounds in God's own character and ways for His people to take and find comfort and encouragement in Him? The present passage focuses on four.

God – the One who hears prayer

Back in verse 44 the people's fear was that prayer was useless: 'You have covered yourself with a cloud so that no prayer can get through.' But, we are thankful to see, they had persevered, in accordance with the vital New Testament principle that we 'should always pray and not give up' (Luke 18:1), and they had found that, true to Himself, God had heard their cry.

The picture in verse 55 is of the people in the remotest depths of misery: 'I called on your name, O Lord, from the depths of the pit.' For 'pit', the AV has 'low dungeon'. The 'personification' of the people continues as the prophet makes their expressions his own. Yet although their prayer and calling upon God was the result of such apparently desperate and hopeless circumstances, the Lord's ear was not 'too dull to hear' (Isaiah 59:1). This is exactly what Jonah found when 'from inside the fish Jonah prayed to the Lord his God' (Jonah 2). And it is exactly what so many of the Lord's people have found continually: however extreme may be their suffering, persecution, tears, despondency or affliction, God delights to hear the voice of His people as they cry to Him.

Indeed, God's people find even more than this! They find that, time and time again, He is more ready to hear than we are to pray. They find the precious promise of Isaiah 65:24 coming true in their own personal experience: 'Before they call I will answer; while they are still speaking I will hear.' And they find, as well, that God 'is able to do immeasurably more than all we ask or imagine' (Ephesians 3:20). Prayer is the language of need, and it is a most blessed assurance that God will not only heed but help – and that in these lavish terms!

Jeremiah continues with verse 56: 'You heard my plea: "Do not close your ears to my cry for relief."' For 'plea' the AV has 'breathing'. 'In prayer we breathe towards God, we breathe after Him,' says Matthew Henry. Or, as James Montgomery puts it in his hymn, 'Prayer is the Christian's vital breath, the Christian's native air.' Those 'breathings' and 'pleas' will often be expressed as cries, groans and sighs – which reminds us of the lovely intercessory ministry of the Holy Spirit described in Romans 8:26-27. This is yet another instance of God's abundant provision for all His people's needs!

Remember that the people of God, the church of Christ, are not to measure the power and grace of God by the limits of their own thoughts and understanding, but are to glorify God by reclining upon Him and relying upon Him even in the worst of extremities. I once found these words in the fly-leaf of an old Bible: 'Pray hardest when it's hardest to pray.' There is an important lesson there. One who was very much an advanced student in the school of prayer was James Hudson Taylor of the China Inland Mission. Writing in just the fourth issue of the magazine *China's Millions,* he observed, 'Want of trust is at the root of almost all our sins and all our weaknesses; and how shall we escape it but by looking to Him and observing His faithfulness?'[1]

Look at verse 57: **'You came near when I called you, and you said, "Do not fear."'** Is not this a lovely illustration of that mutual drawing near of which James speaks in his letter: 'Come near to God and he will come near to you'? (James 4:8). Here are the nearness, the love, the sympathy, the deliverance, the graciousness, the promptness, the tenderness and the sweetness of God all rolled into one. Someone has observed, helpfully, that the prayers to God of His children are not the cries of orphans in an empty house without a father to hear or answer! Blessed be His name! Here is the ever-open refuge of which we have to say, to our shame, we still know all too little.

It was once the experience of a Christian to be caught in a snowstorm that drove his boat onto part of the Scottish coast. His comrades struck up a dirge to the effect that 'The snowstorm closes the road along the shore and the storm bars our way over the sea,' to which the brother in question responded, 'There is still the way of heaven; that lies open.'

God – the Redeemer of our life

This follows on from what we have just seen, for it was as the Redeemer of His people that God revealed Himself in answer to their prayers. One of the most blessed and lasting effects upon God's people, as Jeremiah and the people knew from experience, is that the knowledge that earlier prayers have been answered supplies strong grounds for hope that in a fresh circumstance of need the Lord will once again prove Himself to be what we have already found Him to be in the past.

So Jeremiah testifies in verse 58, **'O Lord, you took up my case; you redeemed my life.'** Keil translates the first phrase of the verse: 'Thou dost conduct the causes of my soul,' and Calvin: 'Thou hast pleaded the pleadings of my soul.' The point, surely, is this: not only are His people bidden to plead to God in their need; they are also assured of His delight in pleading their cause. He can be depended upon thoroughly. Many friends at different times will put themselves out for us and seek to come to our aid or defence, but they do not always succeed. Sometimes they cannot help us, despite their best efforts and intentions. But with God the situation is different. 'God', says Calvin, 'is such a pleader of our cause that He is also a deliverer, for our safety is in His hand.'

'You redeemed my life,' says Jeremiah. God comes with redemption. He comes with deliverance – such that when it appears that all is lost, He is the *'Goel'*, the 'Kinsman-Redeemer', who is pleased to draw near to His people and rescue them from their troubles. David testified along the same lines in Psalm 34:4-6, 19-22. Meditate afresh on Toplady's rich lines:

A Sovereign Protector I have,
  Unseen, yet for ever at hand,
Unchangeably faithful to save,
  Almighty to rule and command.
He smiles, and my comforts abound;
  His grace as the dew shall descend;
And walls of salvation surround
  The soul He delights to defend.

Inspirer and Hearer of prayer,
  Thou Shepherd and Guardian of Thine,
My all to Thy covenant care
  I sleeping and waking resign.
If thou art my Shield and my Sun,
  The night is no darkness to me;
And fast as my moments roll on,
  They bring me but nearer to Thee.

Kind Author, and ground of my hope,
  Thee, Thee, for my God I avow;
My glad Ebenezer set up,
  And own Thou hast helped me till now.
I muse on the years that are past,
  Wherein my defence Thou hast proved;
Nor wilt Thou relinquish at last
  A sinner so signally loved!

God – the all-seeing One

Verses 59-63 breathe the spirit of great confidence in God, and with good reason. Lamentations has been full of the grievous treatment of God's people by their (and His) enemies and references to that abound here: **'the wrong done to me'** (3:59); **'the depth of their vengeance'** (3:60 – the word may mean vindictiveness, or acts of violence or cruelty); **'their plots'** (3:60); **'their insults'** (3:61); all the things **'my enemies whisper and mutter against me all day long'** (3:62) and their mocking songs (3:63). All of these 'summaries' can be filled out from earlier portions of the book.

But where is the encouragement and confidence to be found by God's people in all this? In the fact that God is the all-seeing One! **'You have seen, O Lord'** (3:59); **'You have seen'** (3:60); **'O Lord, you have heard'** (3:61); **'Look at them!'** (3:63).

Jeremiah is able to make his plea to God's justice because he knows that God sees and hears all that happens. Nothing escapes His attention, whether large or small, public or private, among His people or at large in the world. While there are times when it can appear that God has forgotten His church, or His child, and left them to the mercy of their oppressors and their afflictions, yet in reality it is not so. Heaven is not indifferent. God recognizes the wrongs done to and suffered by His people. Indeed, more than that, in all their afflictions He is afflicted (cf. Isaiah 63:9). He takes note of every act of injustice and wrong and He registers every pang of suffering. He is aware of all the cruel plottings and malicious reproaches of His people's enemies; and how vain and foolish their opposition must appear to Him, for in a moment He can shatter all their schemes and silence their revilings for ever!

What a gigantic cause of encouragement in God this should be! And we greatly need it, for our weak flesh and our failing hearts, even in the face of light trials, so quickly start arguing wrongly or leaping to false conclusions that God has forsaken us or that He does not love us any more. We need a strong dose of the exhortation, 'Begone, unbelief!', and should be stirred to courage in our trials and patience to wait for God to deliver us from our trials, for He sees and He knows all things, and at the right time He will come to our aid. Isaiah 40:27 is right on cue here:

'Why do you say, O Jacob,
    and complain, O Israel,
"My way is hidden from the Lord;
    My cause is disregarded by my God"?'

– and be sure not to miss the verses that follow it!

Let me add a note on verse 63, which gives a sad picture of God's enemies making themselves merry with His people's miseries and having a good laugh at their expense. Harrison tells us that mocking songs or taunt songs were used frequently in the Ancient Near East to express derision or contempt for an enemy, and cites Numbers 21:27-30, Isaiah 47:1-15 and Habakkuk 2:6-19 as examples.

God – the Vindicator

In the closing verses of chapter 3 we have a reflection of the glorious truth of Psalm 37:5-7, where David says,

'Commit your way to the Lord;
   trust in Him and He will do this:
He will make your righteousness shine like the dawn,
   the justice of your cause like the noonday sun.
Be still before the Lord and wait patiently for Him;
   do not fret when men succeed in their ways,
   when they carry out their wicked schemes.'

What is Jeremiah doing in verses 64-66? Nothing less than calling for God to take vengeance upon His enemies. Follow it through in the three verses.

'Pay them back what they deserve, O Lord, for what their hands have done' (3:64). The vengeance Jeremiah calls for is 'what they deserve'; it is 'for what their hands have done'. In other words, it is a matter of divine justice so far as the prophet is concerned. Sin must be punished. Those who are evildoers and who set themselves up against the Lord and against His people must be dealt with by God.

'Put a veil over their hearts' (3:65) (AV 'give them sorrow of heart') is strictly a reference to spiritual blindness, leading to obstinacy and hardness, and that in turn to God's curse: **'And may your curse be on them!'**

God is the inescapable God and, so that His enemies will be in no doubt concerning that fact, the prophet cries in verse 66, **'Pursue them in anger and destroy them from under the heavens of the Lord.'** 'The heavens of the Lord' is a reference to the whole world, over all of which God's authority extends, and so the call is nothing less than to 'exterminate them wholly from the sphere of Thy dominion in the world'.[2] There is no escape for the workers of iniquity anywhere 'under the heavens of the Lord'.

To say that Jeremiah is speaking in strong terms is partly to state the obvious and partly to make an understatement. Is it a right way to pray? And does it conflict with, say, New Testament teaching on our relationship towards our enemies? We made some remarks upon this question in connection with 1:21-22, but it may be in order to add one or two further reflections at this point.

Certainly we are exhorted by the Lord Jesus Christ, 'Love your enemies, do good to those who hate you, bless those who curse you, pray for those who ill-treat you' (Luke 6:27-28), and in laying that upon the line He is giving us an order, not an option. We might add, moreover, that His own example is absolutely consistent with His teaching (Luke 23:34). However, when God's people pray as Jeremiah prays here, there is not a contradiction with New Testament teaching. How is that? Because it is not violent feelings, passionate hatred or desires after bloodthirsty revenge that motivate such praying – at least, it never should be those things – but, in Calvin's phrase, 'pure zeal and rightly formed'. The Christian is very genuinely concerned that even the most furious opponents of the gospel – indeed especially such! – be converted, that they become like little children and enter the kingdom of heaven. But the Christian is also very genuinely concerned for the honour and justice of God, and, with thorough consistency, may therefore pray with Jeremiah here, or with David in Psalm 68:1-3, where he says, 'May God arise, may his enemies be scattered; may his foes flee before him.' And, of course, if God's enemies are not converted, there only remains for them that full, final and righteous outpouring of His wrath which at the end of the day divine justice is certain to render.

One final comment: 'The Lord is the Supreme Ruler and Judge, in spite of all efforts to dethrone Him.'[3] So the apparent divine patience with evildoers, as God withholds judgement from them, or His apparent unconcern for His people, as He withholds deliverance from them, are not indications of His indifference either to the one or the other. He will bring judgement upon His enemies and deliverance to His people.

His justice and His grace assure us so. Have you realized that clearly? Then what difference does it make to your life?

9.
Former glories

Please read Lamentations 4:1-11

We all like to look back to the good old days, even if at the time they did not seem quite so wonderful. And with the passing of kingdoms and empires, as well as when we look back fondly and longingly to sweet seasons of revival in past days, it is customary to think of the former glories, the glories that used to be, 'the glory that was'. The whole subject of this next section of Lamentations, as we move into chapter 4, is set out along these lines. The happy condition of former days in the life of the people of God is contrasted with the present state of humiliation and judgement. Everything and everyone has been affected. There is an appalling sweep to these verses. And the dominant note that comes through is this: the calamity that had overtaken Judah and Jerusalem was a well-merited punishment by God.

The people of Zion

Jeremiah is speaking metaphorically here when he speaks of **'how the gold has lost its lustre, the fine gold become dull'**. It is not the city itself, the temple buildings, walls and so on, that he is meaning, but the people themselves. It is they who are likened to gold and sacred gems.

Gold is a familiar emblem of very worthy people and **'sacred gems'** are precious stones intended for sacred purposes. The two expressions taken together form a figurative description of the people of Israel – indeed the people of God at all times and in every generation – as 'a chosen people, a royal priesthood, a holy nation, a people belonging to God' (1

Peter 2:9; cf. Exodus 19:5-6). The **'sons of Zion'** are **'precious'** (or dear) to God and **'worth their weight in gold'**. But now, with Jerusalem destroyed, they are **'considered as pots of clay, the work of a potter's hands'**.

The gold – not least the glory and brightness of the people, by the very fact of being the people of God – has lost its glitter and lustre. **'The sacred gems are scattered at the head of every street.'** In other words, having been brought down by the Lord because of all their grievous sins, they now mingle without distinction among everyone else, having lost all their esteem and being treated with utter contempt. Their description as 'pots of clay' (AV 'earthen pitchers') gives the sense of ignoble materials made by human hands and easily smashed to pieces. Israel was among the nations what gold is among the metals and precious stones are among minerals. But how things have changed! No longer do they bear any resemblance to their former beauty and holiness.

The children

In having to bear their part in the effects of God's punishment, the children were receiving worse treatment than the offspring of jackals or the fledglings of an ostrich. **'Even jackals offer their breasts to nurse their young, but my people have become heartless like ostriches in the desert.'** The ostrich had a reputation for cruelty and indifference to the needs of its young, as is indicated in a vivid portion in the book of Job:

> 'She lays her eggs on the ground
>   and lets them warm in the sand,
> unmindful that a foot may crush them,
>   that some wild animal may trample them.
> She treats her young harshly, as if they were not hers;
>   she cares not that her labour was in vain ... '
>   (Job 39:14-16).

On this account the Arabs often called the ostrich the 'impious' or 'ungodly' bird.

Because of the famine (2:11-12,19) the nursing mothers were no longer able to satisfy the hunger cravings of their starving children. These verses are pathetic and desperate. Jeremiah could not get the picture out of his mind. **'Because of thirst the infant's tongue sticks to the roof of its mouth; the children beg for bread, but no one gives it to them.'**

The adults

Here again, in verses 5 and 6, we find evidence of the great turn-around following upon the people's disobedience to God. And once more the language of contrast is striking: **'Those who once ate delicacies are destitute in the streets. Those nurtured in purple now lie on ash heaps.'** All luxuries, all fineries, all standing on ceremony has been stripped away, and it is an understatement even to say that the people are down to the bare essentials. They are lying destitute on the streets. They are lying on ash heaps (AV, they 'embrace dunghills'), maybe even scratching about there in hope of finding some morsel to sustain them.

How can such a punishment be described? With what can you compare it? The prophet announces that **'The punishment of my people is greater than that of Sodom.'** Sodom became proverbial for its wickedness, and the Lord's destruction of it is recorded in Genesis 19: 'Then the Lord rained down burning sulphur on Sodom and Gomorrah – from the Lord out of the heavens. Thus he overthrew those cities and the entire plain, including all those living in the cities – and also the vegetation in the land' (Genesis 19:24-25; cf. 27-28). Recalling this, we might be prompted to wonder how it can be that Jerusalem's punishment is a greater one. The clue is there in verse 6 itself. Sodom **'was overthrown in a moment'**, but Jerusalem, 'for her far more serious crime of rejecting covenant mercies ... must seemingly endure a proportionately greater chastisement'.[1] There is no question about it. It was the Lord who inflicted the punishment in both cases. But, as Matthew Henry comments, 'Sodom never had the means of grace that Jerusalem had, the oracles of God and His prophets.' The suggestion is not that there are degrees of sin – for sin as sin is abhorrent to God in His holiness – but that Jerusalem had tasted so much of the Lord that her sin was more horrendous in His sight. While Sodom's judgement was over in a moment, Jerusalem, to quote Matthew Henry again, 'came down slowly, and died a lingering death'.

The phrase concerning Sodom at the end of verse 6, **'without a hand turned to help her'** (AV 'and no hands stayed on her'), is a difficult one to translate because of a measure of uncertainty over the root of the verb. One suggested rendering is 'with no hands trembling in it' – the sense being that the inhabitants of Sodom were taken completely by surprise, unaware of their impending destruction, whereas God had warned His people Judah over and over again.

The nobles

The AV speaks of 'Nazirites' in verse 7 (cf. Numbers 6; Judges 13), but **'princes'** is better, or it could be translated 'distinguished ones', for the term denotes those conspicuous because of their rank. Again, the contrast between former glories and present humiliations stands to the fore. **'Their princes were brighter than snow and whiter than milk, their bodies more ruddy than rubies, their appearance like sapphires'** (4:7). But compare that picture of dignity, purity, holiness and beauty with what follows in verse 8. **'But now they are blacker than soot; they are not recognized in the streets. Their skin has shrivelled on their bones; it has become as dry as a stick.'** 'Blacker than soot' could be translated 'darker than blackness' – that is to say, with every last trace of beauty and splendour vanished, such that they are unrecognizable in the street as they walk along looking like skeletons. The flowers of society, the leaders among the people, have become as nothing at all. How are the mighty fallen!

The mothers

We have seen something of their calamity already, as they are unable to feed their children (4:3-4). But what is revealed here reaches more horrifying depths still. Women, known for their compassionate spirits and deep love for their children, now **'with their own hands ... have cooked their own children'** and eaten them for food. We had a reference to this back in 2:20.[2]

What then is the explanation, not only for the plight of the mothers of children, but for all that has been recorded so far in chapter 4? The answer is clear: **'The Lord has given full vent to his wrath; he has poured out his fierce anger'** (4:11). Oh, the terror of God's wrath! Who can abide it? Instead of leading nations in the ways of divine truth – which is what she should have been doing – Judah was herself experiencing both the *awfulness* and the *awesomeness* of divine judgement. 'The scenes of horror which have been depicted show the meeting-place of Zion's guilt and its Divine punisher. God's fierce wrath is the blast which consumes flagrant iniquities.'[3] The greatness of Zion's guilt is matched by the measure of the divine wrath. And this is underscored in the surprising detail given in the second part of verse 11: **'He kindled a fire in Zion that consumed her foundations.'** Fire usually takes hold of roofs and the contents of buildings, but here God has 'kindled a fire in Zion that consumed her foundations' – a judgement, that is, that has got right below the surface and penetrated to the very foundations of life. What a metaphor for the fulness and the completeness of God's visitation in judgement!

A number of abiding applications arise from this passage, and I can only suggest some of them. Let me cast them in the form of four 'reminders'.

1. The first is that, in New Testament terms, 'From everyone who has been given much, much will be demanded, and from the one who has been entrusted with much, much more will be asked' (Luke 12:48). George Barlow has expressed the way this works out so eloquently that it will be better if I give it in his words rather than try to paraphrase it in my own: 'Judah was a choice and consecrated nation, and enjoyed unexampled privileges. She was raised not only into temporal affluence and splendour, but was intended to represent the lofty type of a moral and spiritual commonwealth. She was the custodian and teacher of spiritual blessings that were to enrich the world. She was the medium through which Jehovah sought to express His gracious purpose of salvation to the whole human race. No nation had been so exalted and so honoured. While she remained faithful to her calling, Judah was supreme and invulnerable among the nations. She shone with the lustre of the most fine gold, and her position was as secure as that of an impregnable fortress. But when she sinned she fell, and her fall was the more notable when contrasted with her former greatness and grandeur.'

The application of this to the church of Christ, which has received so much privilege and so much blessing, and has been charged with the guarding and proclaiming of the gospel, and the application of this to each individual Christian stands out plainly. God requires certain things of all His creatures, for He is their Maker and the One who gives them 'life and breath and everything else' (Acts 17:25). But how much more does He require, in terms of holiness, obedience, devotion, faithfulness, single-mindedness, perseverance and the like, of those who belong to Him through the payment of the ransom price of the blood of His Son? The sin of the people of God is always the greatest and always the worst, for it is the grossest abuse imaginable of the revelation, blessings and grace of God. 'What shall we say, then? Shall we go on sinning, so that grace may increase? By no means! We died to sin; how can we live in it any longer? (Romans 6:1-2).

2. Secondly, we should not rest on any laurels or take the presumptuous view that 'Because God has blessed us in the past He is bound to bless us in the future,' or 'Because I have been used in the past I will be sure to be used again', regardless of how we conduct ourselves, no matter what the church does, or how the Christian behaves, or how careless we become over prayer, holiness, and so on.

Rather, says the apostle Paul, 'Conduct yourselves in a manner worthy of the gospel of Christ' (Philippians 1:27); 'Continue to work out your salvation with fear and trembling' (Philippians 2:12). We, who have been so richly endowed with the gospel, need to take special and continual care that, with the Lord's help, in all things we walk worthily of the gospel and of the Lord.

3. The third reminder is of the perishable and passing nature of the 'splendours' of the world, and the danger of trusting in riches – or, for that matter, in any externals. Look where it got these people – those who had looked so fine and

possessed such dignity and honour had it all taken away and became 'as dry as a stick'.

The words of the Lord Jesus Christ deserve careful meditation: 'Do not store up for yourselves treasures on earth, where moth and rust destroy, and where thieves break in and steal. But store up for yourselves treasures in heaven, where moth and rust do not destroy, and where thieves do not break in and steal. For where your treasure is, there your heart will be also' (Matthew 6:19-21).

Nothing is safe where righteousness and holiness are ignored – whether by individuals, churches or nations.

4. Finally, when God withdraws because His people have been disobedient, or because a nation has followed pell-mell after sin, the most appalling degradation follows – spiritual, political, economic and moral – in the same way that when God revives His church the effects are felt way beyond the boundaries of the church and the whole nation is affected. That degradation is all the more evident and miserable when, as here, it is compared with a former condition of excellence, purity and God's presence and power.

Jeremiah cared so much about the whole situation that he could not lament sufficiently over it – his grief knew no exhaustion. In our day, in our generation, in our calamities that surround us on every side: do *we* weep? Do *we* care?

10.
It could never happen to us!

Please read Lamentations 4:12-22

It could never happen to us! We must all have said that at one time or another of situations in our personal lives, in our family, church or nation. Whatever has happened to others could never happen to us! And how often have we been proved wrong, and in a costly and humbling manner!

The second part of chapter 4 begins with an expression of utter amazement that judgement – the judgement of Jehovah, the covenant God – could ever have happened to Judah and Jerusalem. Yet this is not only a matter of amazement, shock, perplexity and horror to the people of God themselves. Verse 12 opens it all out onto a wider plane: **'The kings of the earth did not believe, nor did any of the world's people, that enemies and foes could enter the gates of Jerusalem.'** Do you see that deliberate emphasis? Even the pagan adversaries of Judah, the ungodly nations round about, described comprehensively in these two phrases as 'the kings of the earth' and 'the world's people', thought Judah was safe and Jerusalem impregnable. But just as the confidence of the citizens of Jerusalem was a false confidence (cf. the attitude of the Jebusites in 2 Samuel 5:6-10), so the imagining of the outsiders was a false imagining. The Lord, it seems, had done what no one thought could be done. His people's (and therefore His own) enemies and foes had entered the gates of Jerusalem, taken the city and exiled the inhabitants. What a sobering reminder that there is on earth no city so secure and no kingdom so powerful and no stronghold so impregnable that it may not be destroyed by sins and unrighteousness! All trust in human 'strongholds' (whatever they are!) is idle.

But, once again, the prophet's concern is not merely to record *what* has happened but to demonstrate *why* this seeming impossibility has happened. He is not looking for scapegoats, for in a sense all the people were at fault. But one factor stands out in particular, and is dealt with first of all.

The unfaithfulness of the religious leaders

This is no new theme in the book, but it is now powerfully emphasized in verses 13-16. The people who, more than any-one else, should have known better – the prophets and the priests – turned out to be the worst of all and are here casti-gated for their sins and iniquities and their persecution of the innocent. Not that it was their fault alone. There was a real sense in which they gave the people what the people them-selves asked for and desired. So the rank and file – the ordi-nary people – are very far from being exonerated. Yet, still, the major failure is laid squarely at the door of those whom God holds chiefly responsible.

And so Jeremiah records, **'But it happened because of the sins of her prophets and the iniquities of her priests'** (4:13). It was the primary duty of the prophets and priests to explain, enforce and uphold the Word of God, whereas in the event they were the prime movers in all the attempts to silence that Word. The Lord had warned them enough times through the course of Jeremiah's ministry. Jeremiah 6:13-15 is a classic example:

"'From the least to the greatest,
    all are greedy for gain;
prophets and priests alike,
    all practise deceit.
They dress the wound of my people
    as though it were not serious.
"Peace, peace", they say,
    when there is no peace.
Are they ashamed of their loathsome conduct?
    No, they have no shame at all;
    they do not even know how to blush.
So they will fall among the fallen;
    they will be brought down when I punish them,"
                                                    says the Lord.'

With this, compare 8:10-12 and 23:9-40. But they paid no
attention to the truly appointed prophet of the Lord, God's
authorized spokesman among them, but had turned to their
own ways, made up their own teaching and followed their
own devices. And, as we have already seen, the tragedy is that
so many others are affected when the blind lead the blind.
The inevitable result is that they all end up falling into the pit
(Matthew 15:14). When God's ministers, who ought to be
captive to His Word and consecrated to His service, become
defiled, then they are a curse and not a blessing, they are reck-
less and ruinous in all they say and do.

What is meant by the reference at the end of verse 13 to the
prophets and priests having **'shed within her the blood of the
righteous'**? By 'her', of course, is meant Jerusalem. Matthew
Henry has a helpful explanation: 'They not only shed the
blood of their innocent children, whom they sacrificed to
Moloch,[1] but the blood of the righteous men that were among
them, whom they sacrificed to that more cruel idol of enmity
to the truth and true religion.' The awful truth is that the
prophets and priests were the ringleaders in this persecution
– just as, we might add, in Christ's day it was the religious
leaders (Pharisees, Sadducees, chief priests and scribes) who
incensed the people against Christ and led them up blind
alleys to the destruction of their souls. This links up with the
famous teaching in Ezekiel 33 about the watchman's concern
for souls. Heed again God's solemn and challenging word in
Ezekiel 33:7-9, where He says, 'Son of man, I have made you
a watchman for the house of Israel; so hear the word I speak,
and give them warning from me. When I say to the wicked,
"O wicked man, you will surely die," and you do not speak
out to dissuade him from his ways, that wicked man will die
for his sin, and I will hold you accountable for his blood. But
if you do warn the wicked man to turn from his ways and he
does not do so, he will die for his sin, but you will be saved
yourself.'

God's judgement upon them is set out in verses 14-16. The
picture in verses 14-15 is that of lepers: **'Now they grope
through the streets like men who are blind. They are so defiled
with blood that no one dares to touch their garments. "Go
away! You are unclean!" men cry to them. "Away! Away!**

Don't touch us!'" They were treated like outcast lepers. The same warnings were given to people to have nothing to do with them as would be proclaimed if a leper – an untouchable – was seen approaching. They had become unclean. No one should touch them. No one should associate with them. No one should take them in. But this was so not only at home, for verse 15 continues, **'When they flee and wander about, people among the nations say, "They can stay here no longer."'** They were shunned even when they went off to find a place of refuge outside their native land, and (in the spirit of Deuteronomy 28:65) were forced to wander around from place to place, seeking rest and refuge and finding none.

And, as in 2:17, Jeremiah again emphasizes whose judgement it is, who is the Author of it: **'The Lord himself has scattered them; he no longer watches over them'**(4:16). As a result, **'The priests are shown no honour, the elders no favour,'** either from the Lord or from men. The AV translates the beginning of verse 16 as 'The anger of the Lord hath divided them.' We might even say, 'the face of the Lord', or 'the countenance of the Lord', for there is no punishment too severe for unfaithful ministers of God's Word.

And this points up the terrible danger and tragedy of becoming a preacher or a minister before becoming a Christian. Richard Baxter remarks of such men: 'They worship an unknown God and proclaim an unknown Christ, and pray through an unknown Spirit, and preach a state of holiness and fellowship with Christ and a glory and a blessedness which are wholly unknown to them, and perhaps will remain unknown through all eternity. He must indeed be a heartless preacher who has not himself in his own heart the Christ and the grace he declares.'

The twentieth-century application of this is plain and can be summed up in three pleas to God:

1.   May God be pleased to deliver us from all such men!

2.   May God give us grace and wisdom to examine our own hearts lest we be such men; let us not be satisfied with what Calvin calls 'naked titles' (whether prophet or priest of old or, nowadays, all the variety of titles that are used - biblical ones like minister, pastor, elder, or unbiblical ones like pope, archbishop, vicar) but rather make sure of hearts that know, fear and serve the Lord.

3. May we be driven to prayer for the purity and power of the pulpit, and that God should raise up men of His sovereign appointment and equipment, men after His own heart, in the church and in the nation.

The last hours of a doomed people

Much has been made already in Lamentations of what was said about Judah among the heathen. Have another look through the book and gather the relevant verses freshly. But now in verses 17-20 we discover what the people said about themselves. Follow it through carefully, point by point.

They acknowledged that their every hope of rescue was disappointed (4:17). Whatever aid they might have hoped for from neighbouring kingdoms did not come. Egypt, for example, which had failed them so often before, did so yet again. **'Moreover, our eyes failed, looking in vain for help; from our towers we watched for a nation that could not save us.'** This is a potent reminder of an unchangeable truth: when we are alienated from God, for whatever reason, literally every reliable source of help is cut off. Why? Because when God *will not* help us, man *cannot* help us. And all such hope that man can help is vain, as the people of Judah learned painfully.

They discovered that every avenue of escape was closely guarded (4:18-19). The enemy pressed then tightly and kept them under siege: **'Men stalked us at every step, so we could not walk in our streets.'** They were under the most stringent control and restriction. And if and when they got away it was no better: **'Our pursuers were swifter than eagles in the sky; they chased us over the mountains and lay in wait for us in the desert.'** The Babylonian armies pursued the refugees relentlessly, speedily and successfully, even to the point of setting up ambushes to capture them in the desert areas in the south of Judah.

They felt a deepening conviction that the end was near (4:18). This seemed fearfully inevitable – what with the spiritual famine, the besiegers advancing against them, disease and famine raging in their midst, divisions and alarms spreading through their ranks and, most significant of all, the Lord's own hand against them. **'Our end was near, our days were numbered, for our end had come.'** It seemed to be a case of just waiting for the end to happen. And, to cap it all, there was something more.

Their king was captured (4:20).**'The Lord's anointed, our very life breath, was caught in their traps.'** It is King Zedekiah who is referred to here. The last king of the house of David (he reigned from 597-586 B.C.), he was a weak and treacherous king who condoned the religious corruption and moral degeneracy of the day and took precious little notice of anything that the prophet Jeremiah had to say. Yet, for all this, he was still 'the Lord's anointed' and, as such, the 'very life breath' of the nation. Calvin makes this comment: 'In short, Jeremiah means that the favour of God was as it were extinguished when the king was taken away, because the happiness of the people depended on the king, and the royal dignity was as it were a sure pledge of the grace and favour of God; hence the blessing of God ceased when the king was taken away from the Jews.'[2]

It is important sometimes to distinguish between the *person* of a sovereign and his *office*. What I mean is this. The authority of rulers is to be recognized as coming from God. There is no question about this, and Romans 13:1-7 is a key passage on the matter. Remember how that chapter opens: 'Everyone must submit himself to the governing authorities, for there is no authority except that which God has established. The authorities that exist have been established by God.' Take a moment now to read the whole section. This principle abides, whatever the personal character of the one who exercises the authority. For example, it does not apply only when the sovereign is a Christian. It applies comprehensively to rule and kingship. And while Acts 5:29 reminds us of those occasions when 'we must obey God rather than men', still the teaching stands firm. Even Saul was 'the Lord's anointed' and was revered in his life and mourned in his death as such by David (1 Samuel 24:6; 2 Samuel 1:14). What happened to Zedekiah, then, was what you might call the last straw for the people. He was caught in the enemy's traps. Jeremiah 52:7-11 records how he was captured in the plain of Jericho while fleeing from Jerusalem. The enemy soldiers took him to Nebuchadnezzar, king of Babylon; his sons were slaughtered before his eyes, as were all the officials of Judah; and then Nebuchadnezzar 'put out Zedekiah's eyes, bound him with bronze shackles and took him to Babylon, where he put him in prison till the day of his death'. The people were shattered. All their hopes and dreams were gone. Look at the second half of verse 20: **'We thought that under his shadow we would live among the nations.'** Once again theirs had been a misplaced hope, looking to the creature and not to the Creator, to man and not to God. So their king had perished.

The fate of those who set themselves against God's people

Matthew Henry gets straight to the heart of the matter in summarizing verses 21 and 22 in this way:
  v.21 An end shall be put to Edom's triumph.
  v.22 An end shall be put to Zion's troubles.
  First of all, *the prophet addresses Edom, the enemy of God.* The Edomites, called here the **'Daughter of Edom'** , had been Judah's bitter adversaries for centuries and had often been the object of prophetic pronouncements of judgement.[3] They were in prominence again just now because after the fall of Jerusalem in 586 B.C. Nebuchadnezzar of Babylon had allotted the rural areas of Judah to them as a reward for not allying with Judah against him. 'Uz' was in the general area of Edom. 'Judah had outdistanced Edom and rose to superior greatness and power. This was the offence Edom could never forgive. She watched the downfall of Judah with a savage delight, and when the catastrophe came, which she did her best to accelerate, she gloated over it with a fiendish joy'[4] (cf. Psalm 137:7).
  But why is Edom bidden to **'rejoice and be glad'**? There is surely more than a touch of irony here. Maybe the prophet's sense is, 'You can rejoice for the moment as much as you please as you view Judah captive and exiled – but your joy will be short-lived and you need not think that you will escape the punishment due for your own sins.' And so we read, **'But to you also the cup will be passed; you will be drunk and stripped naked.'** Edom may have been taken up and used by God as an

instrument for His righteous purpose of chastising His own
disobedient and idolatrous people; but she herself as a pagan
and ungodly nation had offended God with her sin and rebellion and would have to face His righteous punishment as
well. She would drink the cup of divine wrath (the 'cup' is a
familiar metaphor in Scripture for adversity and suffering)
and would rock and reel and stagger like a drunken and naked
figure, stripped of all her vaunted power, pride and glory.
Laetsch observes that the last remnant of Edom perished during the siege of Jerusalem, in the early years of the Christian
church (A.D. 70-71).

I am sure it is also valid, in the fulness of Scripture, to see
a wider application of the words used here against Edom to all
the enemies of God's people. There is a sense, in other words,
in which Edom is the representative of them all. Psalm 2 is
brought to mind:

'Why do the nations conspire
    and the peoples plot in vain?
The kings of the earth take their stand
    and the rulers gather together against the Lord
    and against his Anointed One.
"Let us break their chains," they say,
"and throw off their fetters."

The One enthroned in heaven laughs;
    the Lord scoffs at them.
Then he rebukes them in his anger
    and terrifies them in his wrath, saying,
"I have installed my king
    on Zion, my holy hill ... "'

Then *the prophet addresses Judah, the people of God.*
There has already been a ray of hope for Judah in verse 21 to
illumine the dark night of her hopelessness. That ray becomes
a little brighter still in verse 22 with what must have been a
most welcome encouragement held out to the people: **'O
Daughter of Zion, your punishment will end; he will not prolong your exile.'** There is an end in prospect to her punishment; it will not go on for ever and ever. When God has
accomplished His purposes in this regard, He lifts His heavy

hand. 'He will not prolong your exile' perhaps captures the sense rather less ambiguously than the AV's 'He will no more carry thee away into captivity.' The point is not (as was to be proved with the further passage of years and generations) that God would never again send the Jewish nation into captivity, because that would not be true. It means rather that their present exile would not be prolonged beyond the limit determined by their guilt. When their iniquity had been punished sufficiently and satisfactorily by the punishment they received, then there would be a return to the land. You could translate the phrase literally: 'He will not add to banish you,' or 'He will not banish you longer.'

In Psalm 34:17,19 David testifies,

'The righteous cry out, and the Lord hears them;
   He delivers them from all their troubles ...
A righteous man may have many troubles,
   but the Lord delivers him from them all.'

But we may broaden this even further and say that God will ultimately deliver the righteous even from the troubles which they have brought upon themselves. He has entered into covenant with His people, and that covenant is 'everlasting ... arranged and secured in every part' (2 Samuel 23:5). He will not, at the last, abandon His own. If they forsake Him (now as then) His people will be chastised until they acknowledge and repent of their apostasy. But He will have pity for His own name's sake. Their sins had brought upon them the anger of the Lord; but He would not contend for ever.

'But, O Daughter of Edom, he will punish your sin and expose your wickedness' (4:22). Notice how, according to Scripture vocabulary, God *covers* sin when he forgives it (Psalm 32:1-5; Isaiah 38:17) and *exposes* (discovers, reveals) it when He punishes it (Job 20:27; Psalm 90:7-8).

Before we pass on into the final chapter of Lamentations, remember the note on which this present section began back in verse 12 – a note of utter surprise. Even 'the kings of the earth' and 'the world's people' could scarcely credit what had happened to the people of God. But God detests sin among His people quite as much as among the people of the world.

So there really was not anything to be surprised about at all!
Will we never learn?

'Consider therefore the kindness and sternness [AV 'goodness and severity'] of God: sternness to those who fell, but
kindness to you, provided that you continue in his kindness.
Otherwise, you will also be cut off' (Romans 11:22).

'Yet I hold this against you: you have forsaken your first
love. Remember the height from which you have fallen!
Repent and do the things you did at first. If you do not repent,
I will come to you and remove your lampstand from its place'
(Revelation 2:4-5).

11.
'We have sinned!'

Please read Lamentations 5:1-16

Unlike the preceding chapters, this final one is not written in the acrostic form, even though it also divides into twenty-two verses. Indeed this fifth chapter is a prayer rather than a lament, and comprises a realistic review of Judah's afflictions, building up to the climax of a confession of sin: **'Woe to us, for we have sinned!'** (5:16). The fact that the chapter begins and ends with prayer is itself a most hopeful sign, for when our troubles begin to bring us to our knees, then there is good reason to hope that comfort and deliverance will not be far off. Spurgeon remarks in this connection that 'Sinking times are praying times with the Lord's servants,' and goes on to say, 'Heaven's great harbour of refuge is All-prayer. Thousands of weather-beaten vessels have found a haven there, and the moment a storm comes on it is wise for us to make for it with all sail.' That is certainly the very haven which Jeremiah makes for here on behalf of the people.

An opening plea

He comes before the Lord once more using the plural 'us' and 'we', acknowledges realistically the disgrace and reproach the people are in, and pleads, **'Remember, O Lord, what has happened to us; look, and see our disgrace'** (5:1). Notice the emphatic sequence of verbs: 'remember ... look ... see' (AV, 'remember ... consider ... behold'). We are reminded of James 5:13: 'Is any one of you in trouble? He should pray.' Although he asks the Lord to 'remember', there is no possibility, of course, that the Lord has forgotten, and Jeremiah does not really think for one moment that He has, even if on occasions things might seem so bad that it appears that He has. Nothing is ever unknown to the Lord, but the prophet is pleading here with God to show by His actions on behalf of His people that He realizes the full extremity of their condition and is prepared to come to their deliverance and to remove their shame.

The word 'disgrace' (AV, 'reproach') is especially chosen. The reason, remember, that the Lord God had taken the people into covenant with Himself was that they might be a glory and an honour to Him: 'Everyone who is called by my name, whom I created for my glory, whom I formed and made' (Isaiah 43:7). 'As, then, it was God's will that the riches of His glory should appear in the people, nothing could have been more inconsistent than that instead of glory they should have nothing but disgrace and reproach.'[1] Jeremiah desired that God be moved by this, and so majors upon it in the way that he does.

An awesome account

Following this powerful headlining of matters in the opening verse, there follows in verses 2-16 a comprehensive review of Judah's afflictions and their effects. These effects can be gathered up for our purposes into four areas: territorial and political, personal, economic and, last but by no means least, spiritual.

1. Territorial and political effects

The catalogue of calamities begins with the sad recording of the fact of what has happened to the land itself: **'Our inheritance has been turned over to aliens, our homes to foreigners'** (5:2). The land was the proud heritage of the Israelites. Go back, for example, to Leviticus 20:24, where God announced, 'But I said to you, "You will possess their land; I will give it to you as an inheritance, a land flowing with milk and honey." I am the Lord your God, who has set you apart from the nations.'

Canaan was God's gift to His people. It had been promised

to Abraham and his descendants long before they had ever taken possession of it. For a time it had looked as if they might never enter it, but God was faithful to His promise and after long years spent wandering around they entered in and the tribes settled down in their allotted inheritance. But it has now been laid desolate and turned over to the invading armies. As a result the people are under subjection to a foreign yoke.

This comes through further in verse 5, which is a difficult one to translate. The NIV has **'Those who pursue us are at our heels'**, and the AV translates it: 'Our heels are under persecution.' You can take it in such a way that you end up with a mixture of the two: 'We are pursued to our very necks,' and the allusion is probably to the then current practice of a victor placing his foot on the neck of his prostrate enemy to symbolize complete subjugation. Calvin describes it as a picture of the 'servile and even disgraceful oppression of the people', remarking that 'Enemies may sometimes be troublesome to us, either before our face or behind our backs or by our sides, but when they so domineer us as to ride on our necks in this kind of insult there is supreme degradation.' Another suggested translation of the same phrase is along the lines: 'Our pursuers kept so close to us as to be holding our necks.'

Verse 6 also continues the theme: **'We submitted to Egypt and Assyria.'** That verb 'we submitted' is literally, 'we gave the hand,' and could carry various meanings, such as to agree; to extend the hand in misery, not feeling able even to ask for help; to obey; to beg; to make the best bargain they could in coming into servitude to the enemy; or to be glad to submit even to the meanest employment, the hardest terms and the sourest livelihood, in order to get bread, that is, if only their basic needs can be secured.

Verse 8 suggests that the brutality and misery of the yoke upon the Judeans was made far worse by their having 'slaves' ruling over them. **'Slaves rule over us, and there is none to free us from their hands.'** This was no small instance of God's severity upon the people. Slaves in Oriental countries sometimes rose to places of power and, once there, were not necessarily very benign. The ones mentioned here were lording it over the people; they had once been underlings and now had become what Laetsch calls 'overbearing, bullying dictators'. He adds, 'To such men the people of God were hopelessly surrendered by the Lord.'[2]

Before moving on I cannot omit Matthew Henry's blessed remark that it is 'the happiness of all God's spiritual Israel' that the heavenly Canaan is an inheritance that can never be seized from them or be turned over to aliens and strangers. We may be thankful that, although earthly possessions are liable to strange and sudden changes, our heavenly inheritance can never be wrested from the faithful (1 Peter 1:3-5).

2. *Personal effects*

Words of anguish come to the fore again. **'We have become orphans and fatherless, our mothers like widows'** (5:3). What a pathetic figure of those who had no one to protect them, no one to provide for them and no one to care for them! This is the result of the devastating war, the merciless capture of Jerusalem and the banishment in exile to a far country of so many thousands of the population.

There follows in verses 10-14 an appalling array of attacks, humiliations and indignities done to the people's bodies.

The physical consequences of hunger (5:10). **'Our skin is hot as an oven, feverish from hunger.'** Their skin had become dried, parched and discoloured – strong expressions for the fever-heat produced by excessive hunger.

The shameful treatment of the women (5:11). **'Women have been ravished in Zion, and virgins in the towns of Judah.'**

The public disgrace of the princes and elders (5:12). The first part of verse 12, **'Princes have been hung up by their hands,'** probably refers not to their dead bodies being hung up, but rather to an agonizing form of torture while they were still living. They were hung up on high poles or stakes to which their hands were tied. It was a shameful and lingering death. The second part of the verse, **'Elders are shown no respect'**, indicates the insolent and disrespectful treatment of the senior men among the people (cf. Leviticus 19:32).

The heavy burdens placed upon the younger ones (5:13). **'Young men toil at the millstones; boys stagger under loads of wood.'** The young men were put to work which was not ordinarily theirs: carrying and turning the hand-mills to grind the

corn for their military masters (work normally done by
women or slaves), and the boys were treated like beasts of
burden, carrying the wood for fuel (for cooking and other
purposes) until they could scarcely bear the load upon their
shoulders.

The total collapse of their common ways of life (5:14). **'The
elders are gone from the city gate; the young men have stopped
their music.'** No more public meetings with the elders and
judges sitting at the gate to dispense justice and judgement
(cf. 2:10), and no more social pastimes or happy occasions.

3. Economic effects

As a direct result of the occupation of the country, even the
barest necessities of life such as drinking water and bread had
to be paid for – even the water that came from their own wells!
**'We must buy the water we drink; our wood can be had only
at a price'** (5:4). And verse 9 underlines the danger to their
lives from marauding Bedouin bands who came and swooped
upon them as they looked for food: **'We get our bread at the
risk of our lives because of the sword in the desert.'**

4. Spiritual effects

Inevitably all of this built up a terrible effect upon the
people's whole spirit. The iron had entered into their soul,
which is eloquently spelled out in verse 15: **'Joy is gone from
our hearts; our dancing has turned to mourning.'** There was
nothing to be happy or glad about any more, no cause for
merriment or delight. All the people could do – and all they
were inclined to do – was to lie down in sorrow.

'The crown has fallen from our head' (5:16). This is a powerful figurative expression for the fact that Judah has lost everything that matters. The crown with which the Lord had
decked His chosen nation had been removed. Not only was
the king taken captive (4:20), but 'the crown' itself had gone
too – the very royal dignity and glory of the people, their distinctive and honourable position, their special ornaments
with which they were adorned, such as the temple and the
priesthood. There was nothing left. 'National dignity and
prestige have been lost because of the persistent rejection of

the covenantal obligations. This image completes the concept of the degradation of Israel, and assesses the cause of her downfall with complete accuracy.'[3]

An open acknowledgement

But once again the question arises 'Why?' The answer is short and simple, but serious and sincere: **'Woe to us, for we have sinned!'** (5:16). They have 'sinned not against a ritual or a code of law, but against a living Person – Maker, Monarch, Father'.[4] This is a genuine confession of sin. Notice the connection between 'woe' and 'sin'. 'All our woes are owing to our own sin and folly,' remarks Matthew Henry. Though, as he did with the statement about 'our inheritance' (5:2), so here again with the fallen crown, he turns our thoughts towards the gospel when he goes on: 'Earthly crowns are fading, falling things; but, blessed be God, there is "a crown of glory that fades not away", that never falls, "a kingdom that cannot be removed".'

We have not yet commented upon verse 7, and now is the place to do so: **'Our fathers sinned and are no more, and we bear their punishment.'** A similar thought is expressed at a couple of points in Jeremiah's prophecy. Have a careful look at Jeremiah 16:10-13 and 32:18. But do not misunderstand. The people of Judah are not alleging in some proud or indignant manner their innocency, blamelessness and purity before the Lord. That could not be, for it would not be true, and they knew it. Rather a connection is being drawn between the sins of their fathers' generation and those of their own. Jeremiah 16 has a particularly potent 'but you' in verse 12. Having established the wickedness of the fathers, by saying, 'It is because your fathers forsook me', the Lord continues, 'But you have behaved more wickedly than your fathers.' The people of whom the prophet is speaking in Lamentations were just as grievous sinners as their fathers. God's punishment of their fathers was just, and so is the punishment of the people now. The summary or crystallizing of the matter is found in a verse like Daniel 9:8: 'O Lord, we and our kings, our princes and our fathers are covered with shame because we have sinned against you.' Fathers and children have both sinned. Fathers and children both bear the punishment.

Laetsch has a useful comment on this: 'Every individual sinner was to be punished for his own sin; but if children continued to walk in the footsteps of their wicked fathers and even excelled them in point of wickedness, then their penalties will increase in keeping with opportunities neglected, precepts and commandments set aside, warnings and repeated judgements deliberately ignored.' That principle remains. And Calvin adds this: 'But these two things well agree together, that God returns the iniquity of the fathers into the bosom of their children, and yet that the children are chastised for their own sins.'

There is one more thing to say. Oh, that our confession of sin, in our day, for our own and our fathers' sins, would be as honest and uncovered as that here, and that it would have the same effect upon us – that of turning our minds and hearts to the throne of grace! The final section of Lamentations, to which we now turn, will show this.

12.
Hope held out

Please read Lamentations 5:17-22

And so we come to the final section of Lamentations. As we do so, we find the prophet Jeremiah turning afresh to God, comforting himself once more in God's covenant changelessness and faithfulness, and pleading again for mercy towards God's people. These last six verses of the book divide into three short sections.

Concern for Zion

The previous section reached its climax with the acknowledgement and confession: 'Woe to us, for we have sinned!' (5:16). Following on directly from that (verse 17 begins, 'Because of this...') verses 17-18 testify further to the people's weakness, their sense of helplessness and hopelessness and lack of vision and their desperate concern and anxiety for Zion: **'Our hearts are faint'**, sinking under their load of heaviness. **'Our eyes grow dim'**, no doubt with all their weeping and sorrow. And on what count? **'For Mount Zion, which lies desolate, with jackals prowling over it.'**

We are subject to all manner of losses and disappointments in life – property, friends, possessions, health, money, comforts, successes and so on. Some losses can be borne better than others, but sincere and devout believers feel worst of all, and sorrow most of all over the loss of beauty and glory from Zion. Is that not so? The decline of true religion, the withdrawing of God's favour, the absence of God's power, the grieving of God's Spirit, the emptiness or coldness of God's worship – these things and their like cause great agony and heartache, great misery and soul-searching, to the hearts of God's people. Or they should do.

Zion's beauty is spoken of in the highest terms in Scripture, as we have observed at different points in the exposition. But now 'Mount Zion … lies desolate, with jackals prowling over it.' 'Jackals' is preferable to 'foxes' (AV). Once peopled with worshippers, who glorified God, Zion has become the haunt of prowling jackals. Jackals live in waste places and keep out of man's way, so their wandering freely all over ruined Zion is a further indication that the worshippers have gone, the worship has ceased and the whole place, in every sense, has been abandoned – not only by man but by God. It is no longer His dwelling-place or the refuge of His people.

These two verses are no sentimental outpouring of grief for the sake of it. They are nothing less than what the circumstances merit. Recalling the language back at the beginning of the book in 1:4 and the surrounding verses, Samuel Rutherford captures the same spirit as he grieves over the state of the church in Scotland in the seventeenth century. Writing in 1637 from Aberdeen to one of his most frequent correspondents, Marion M'Naught, he pours out his heart: 'Oh, that I may wait for Him till the morning of this benighted kirk [church] break out! This poor, afflicted kirk had a fair morning, but her night came upon her before her noon-day, and she was like a traveller forced to take house in the morning of his journey. And now her adversaries are the chief men in the land; her ways mourn; her gates languish; her children sigh for bread; and there is none to be instant with the Lord, that He would come again to His house, and dry the face of His weeping spouse, and comfort Zion's mourners who are waiting for Him.' Yet he is not hopeless. For he adds, 'I know that He will make corn to grow upon the top of His withered Mount Zion again.'[1]

When did you last hear anyone expressing concern for Zion in those sorts of terms? By and large there seems to be in these days either a complete failure to realize just what an awful state the church is in, or else a comparative unconcern over that state, coupled with a vain imagining that a few human gimmicks, star-turns and strategies will put things right, when what is really needed is nothing less than a powerful divine visitation from on high. Oh, that God would come down! Or, as Isaiah puts it, 'Oh, that you would rend the heavens and come down, that the mountains would tremble before you!' (Isaiah 64:1 – and go on as well to read the verses that follow).

What a message this book of Lamentations is for our own day! How much, to use that strange contemporary phrase, 'it speaks to us where we are'! Since religious declension is invariably at the heart of national decay, no less in our own day and land than for Judah and its people in the seventh and sixth centuries B.C., a truly repentant people needs to be led to mourn over the state of Zion, the church of God and her present forsaken and humiliated condition.

Comfort in God

What we have just been considering in verses 17-18 leads directly to the prophet's emphatic declaration in verse 19: **'You, O Lord, reign for ever; your throne endures from generation to generation.'** Jeremiah raises his eyes to look up to God, and as for him, so for us, the unchanging character and attributes of God should be our never-ceasing source of comfort. It was the same for the psalmist: 'I lift up my eyes to you, to you whose throne is in heaven. As the eyes of slaves look to the hand of their master, as the eyes of a maid look to the hand of her mistress, so our eyes look to the Lord our God, till he shows us his mercy' (Psalm 123:1-2). 'Ignorance of God – ignorance both of His ways and of the practice of communion with Him – lies at the heart of much of the church's weakness today.'[2] What we so urgently need is a grander and fresher view of His sovereignty and eternity as part and parcel of a grander and fresher view of the Lord God in His entirety. The throne of Judah had fallen, but not the throne of God – that throne which Matthew Henry describes as 'the throne of glory, grace and government', unchangeable and immovable.

The Lord reigns for ever. The Lord's throne 'endures from generation to generation'. That is because He Himself is God 'from everlasting to everlasting' and is His people's 'dwelling-place throughout all generations' (Psalm 90:1-2). Enemies may indeed destroy the temple made with hands, but they are all of them powerless to do any harm to the kingdom of the One who inhabits eternity! Indeed the verb 'reign' (5:19; AV 'remain') is literally 'sit' – a further indication of the firmness of God 'who does not change like shifting shadows' (James 1:17).

You could paraphrase Jeremiah's thought here like this: 'Your dwelling-place, O Lord, has become the habitation of the jackals, but You Yourself have not changed. All manner of shakings and disturbances have affected us and the nations round about, but You Yourself remain the same. We seem to have lost everything that You, our covenant God, have ever given to us, but that has not in any way changed You. You reign. Your throne endures. And so we, Your people, cry to You.'

> The Lord Jehovah reigns;
>   His throne is built on high,
> The garments He assumes
>   Are light and majesty:
> His glories shine with beams so bright
> No mortal eye can bear the sight.
>
> The thunders of His hand
>   Keep the wide world in awe;
> His wrath and justice stand
>   To guard His holy law;
> And where His love resolves to bless,
> His truth confirms and seals the grace.
>
> Through all His mighty works
>   Amazing wisdom shines,
> Confounds the powers of hell,
>   And breaks their dark designs;
> Strong is His arm, and shall fulfil
> His great decrees and sovereign will.
>
> And will this mighty King
>   Of glory condescend?
> And will He write His Name
>   My Father and my Friend?
> I love His Name, I love His Word,
> Join all my powers to praise the Lord.

(Isaac Watts).

Craving for God

The passion of the pleading heightens in these closing verses of the book. As Laetsch puts it, 'Having poured out his sorrow, Jeremiah now turns to the Lord in a last fervent appeal.' Let us take it closely, verse by verse.

In verse 20, two earnest questions stand side by side about God forgetting and God forsaking His people: **'Why do you always forget us? Why do you forsake us so long?'** For the majority of the Jews then living, the seventy years of the exile (Jeremiah 25:11) seemed like never-ending, perpetual, lifelong captivity. There seemed no light at all on the horizon – as so often seems to be the case when we are undergoing trial or experiencing affliction or chastisement. It was so easy then, just as it is so easy now, in such circumstances, to start imagining that God had forgotten them and forsaken His people. But Jeremiah, as it were, checks himself immediately, as is indicated in the next verse.

His encouragement that God has not forgotten and will not forsake His people is back in proper perspective in verse 21, not least in the light of the assurance he had been rejoicing over in verse 19 concerning God and His throne and kingdom.

'Restore us to yourself, O Lord, that we may return' (AV, 'Turn thou us unto thee, O Lord, and we shall be turned') implies a clear acknowledgement that the cause of difficulty and distance between God and His people lay with them and not with Him. It always does. They had turned away from Him.

Repentance is a complete turning about, involving a radical change of mind, heart and will. Just think of the lost son in Jesus' famous parable (Luke 15:11-32) who exemplifies these three aspects of repentance. First, 'He came to his senses,' and confessed, 'I have sinned' (change of mind). Then he went further, realizing the nature of his sin: 'Father, I have sinned against heaven and against you. I am no longer worthy to be called your son' (change of heart). But things did not even stop there, for the logical and necessary conclusion of it all was, '"I will set out and go back to my father ..." So he got up and went to his father' (change of will). And we know the blessed end of the story, as he met his father running towards him with outstretched arms and loving kisses, and a lavish, even though wholly undeserved, welcome home!

The people, then, had turned away from God. So it was they who needed to turn back again to Him. Nothing could be a substitute for that, since for so long now the whole course of their lives had been in the direction of wandering further and further from Him and so coming more and more under His judgement.

But in the very language of the prophet there is a clear recognition of inability. They are weak. They cannot return in their own strength. Which of us can? For repentance – although *we* are to repent – is part and parcel of the gift of God. We need His grace to work in us both to will and to do.

And Jeremiah goes on in the same vein in the second part of verse 21. **'Renew our days as of old,'** he pleads. He expresses here a longing that they might all walk in the light with the Lord again and that He would grant to them once more that state of life and grace and blessing that they had enjoyed in former times. It is not merely a request for restoration to their native land. That is involved, of course, for the country of Judah, the city of Jerusalem, the temple, the priesthood, the prophetic office and the monarchy were all important expressions of the covenant relationship between God and His people. But Jeremiah is not viewing these things here in some empty, formal, superstitious way, or for their own sakes. He is not craving for the form of godliness without the power (2 Timothy 3:5). The people long to be true worshippers of the Lord again, in both heart and life.

The sentence carries on from verse 21 into verse 22: **'Renew our days as of old unless you have utterly rejected us and are angry with us beyond measure.'** Does Jeremiah believe that God has 'utterly rejected' His people? Surely not, for he, of all people, is very aware that the Lord God is not only the covenant-making God, but also the covenant-keeping God. He cannot believe that God's restoring mercy will never come.

Utter rejection would be completely incompatible with God's Name, I AM WHO I AM (Exodus 3:14), and His promise (cf. Jeremiah 27:19-22; 29:10-14). And God heard the cry and kept His word and His covenant. At the end of seventy years the Jews were restored to their own land and God came to His people again.

And so the book of Lamentations comes to an end.[3] But the final note is not really a lament or a cry of despair, even if it looks rather like one. Rather there is here a significant strain of hope. There is repentance and there is prayer – and there must be both of these if things are to be put right between God and His people. But when there is repentance and when there is prayer, there is also hope. 'God never leaves any till they first leave Him, nor stands afar off any longer than while they stand afar off from Him,' says Matthew Henry, and goes on to add, 'Those that repent and do their first works shall rejoice and recover their first comforts.'

Both in biblical history and also in church history down the years since, a clear connection can be traced between prayer and revival – with the prayer involving, as a most important ingredient, repentance and mourning over sin. Listen to James: 'Come near to God and he will come near to you. Wash your hands, you sinners, and purify your hearts, you double-minded. Grieve, mourn and wail. Change your laughter to mourning and your joy to gloom. Humble your-selves before the Lord, and he will lift you up' (James 4:8-10).

There is no doubt that the church of God, in so many respects, is a great grief to God in our day. So the note of repentance needs to be sounded strongly. Think of Jeremiah 6:16:

'This is what the Lord says:
"Stand at the crossroads and look;
     ask for the ancient paths,
ask where the good way is, and walk in it,
     and you will find rest for your souls."'

Repentance was so crucial then. Repentance is so crucial now. The more grievous and dark things are, the more earnestly and urgently must the Lord be sought. And through the new and living way opened up for us through the Lord Jesus Christ, He may be sought and He may be found, now as then. We have the assurance of this in Jeremiah's prophecy itself: '"You will seek me and find me when you seek me with all your heart. I will be found by you," declares the Lord, "and will bring you back from captivity. I will gather you from all the nations and places where I have banished you," declares the Lord, "and will bring you back to the place from which I carried you into exile"' (Jeremiah 29:13-14).

I was very struck with this comment from the commentator Scott, and record it here as we draw to a close: 'Various tribulations may make our hearts faint and our eyes dim: but our way to the mercy-seat of our reconciled God still is open; and we may beseech Him not to forsake or forget us, and plead with Him to turn and renew us more and more by His grace; that our hopes may revive and our consolations abound as in days of old. For the eternal and unchangeable God will not utterly reject His church or any true believer, whatever our trials, fears or lamentations may be. Let us then, in all our troubles, put our whole trust and confidence in His mercy; let us confess our sins and pour out our hearts before Him; and let us watch against repinings or despondency, whatever we suffer or witness of the trouble of our brethren. For this we surely know, that it shall be well in the event with all who trust, fear, love and serve the Lord.'[4]

After all the darkness, all the lamentation, all the gloom that we have found throughout so much of the book, you can see that, as hope begins to spring up at the very end, the book of Lamentations ends on a very positive and encouraging note with respect to God's dealings with His church and people. And what a blessed assurance that is to our souls! Even the most cloudy morning can bring forth the most shining day!

Appendix I

Thomas Brooks on 'The Lord is my portion'

In his treatise *An Ark for all God's Noahs*,[1] Thomas Brooks, one of the choicest ministers of the Puritan age, expounds Lamentations 3:24, and in particular the testimony there: 'The Lord is my portion.'

Under his first main division, 'What a portion the Lord is to His saints, to His gracious ones,' he draws attention to no less than fifteen features. As His people's portion God is present; immense; all-sufficient; absolute, needful and necessary; pure and universal; glorious, happy and blessed; peculiar; universal; safe and secure; suitable; incomprehensible; inexhaustible; soul-satisfying; permanent, indefinite, never-failing, everlasting; and, finally, incomparable.

Later he goes on to set out the grounds of our title to God as our portion. They are threefold: the free favour and love of God, the covenant of grace, and marriage union. He then applies the truth that God is our portion (fourteen points here!). Nor is he unmindful of vital practical questions, such as 'How shall we know whether God be our portion?' and the matter of how we make God our portion.

The whole treatise is most warmly recommended to all for its richness, fulness and closeness of application. This is some of the Puritan preaching at its best! Here is one brief taste.

'Oh how should the saints, that have God for their portion, make their boast of their God, and rejoice in their God, and glory in their God! Shall the men of the world glory in an earthly portion, and shall not a saint glory in his heavenly portion? Shall they glory in a portion that they have only in hope, and shall not a Christian glory in that portion that he hath already in hand? Shall they glory in a portion that they have

only in reversion, and shall not a saint glory in that portion
that he hath in present possession? Shall they glory in their
hundreds and thousands a year, and shall not a Christian
glory in that God that fills heaven and earth with His glory? In
all the Scriptures there is no one duty more pressed than this,
of rejoicing in God; and indeed, if you consider God as a
saint's portion, there is everything in God that may encourage
the soul to rejoice in Him, and there is nothing in God that
may in the least discourage the soul from rejoicing and glory-
ing in Him.'

Appendix II

John Calvin's prayers

John Calvin gave eighteen consecutive lectures on the book of Lamentations in the course of his regular ministry in Geneva. Not surprisingly, he ended each lecture with prayer. These prayers are noteworthy for two reasons. In the first place, they are in a sense model prayers. But the second reason, and the particularly interesting one from our point of view, is that they are choice examples of turning Scripture directly into prayer and a reminder of the effect the Word of God should have on us in fuelling our prayer. In a remarkable manner each of these brief prayers gathers up and crystallizes the teaching of the passage that Calvin and his hearers had just been studying.

I am reproducing five of the prayers here, one for each chapter of Lamentations.

After 1:10: Grant, Almighty God, that as at this day we see Thy church miserably afflicted, we may direct our eyes so as to see our own sins, and so humble ourselves before Thy throne, that we may yet cease not to entertain hope, and in the midst of death wait for life; and may this confidence open our mouth, that we may courageously persevere in calling on Thy name. Through Christ our Lord, Amen.

After 2:14: Grant, Almighty God, that though Thou chastisest us as we deserve, we may yet never have the light of truth extinguished among us, but may ever see, even in darkness, at least some sparks, which may enable us to behold Thy paternal goodness and mercy, so that we may especially be humbled under Thy mighty hand, and that being really prostrate through a deep feeling of repentance, we may raise our hopes to heaven, and never doubt but that Thou wilt at length be reconciled to us when we seek Thee in Thine only-begotten Son. Amen.

After 3:23: Grant, Almighty God, that as there are none of us who have not continually to contend with many temptations, and as such is our infirmity that we are ready to succumb under them, except Thou helpest us – Oh, grant that we may be sustained by Thine invincible power, and that also, when Thou wouldest humble us, we may loathe ourselves on account of our sins, and thus perseveringly contend, until, having gained the victory, we shall give Thee the glory for Thy perpetual aid in Christ Jesus our Lord! Amen.

After 4:22: Grant, Almighty God, that as Thou seest that at this day the mouths not only of our enemies, but of Thine also, are open to speak evil – Oh, grant that no occasion may be given them, especially as their slanders are cast on Thy holy name; but restrain Thou their insolence, and so spare us, that though we deserve to be chastised, Thou mayest yet have regard for Thine own glory, and thus gather us under Christ our Head, and restore Thy scattered church, until we shall at length be all gathered into that celestial kingdom, which Thine only-begotten Son our Lord has procured for us by His own blood. Amen.

After 5:22: Grant, Almighty God, that as Thou didst formerly execute judgements so severe on Thy people – Oh, grant that these chastisements may at this day teach us to fear Thy name, and also keep us in watchfulness and humility, and that we may so strive to pursue the course of our calling that we may find that Thou art always our leader, that Thy hand is stretched forth to us, that Thy aid is ever ready for us, until, being at length gathered into Thy celestial kingdom, we shall enjoy that eternal life, which Thine only-begotten Son has obtained for us by His own blood. Amen.

References

Introducing Lamentations
1. Two books by Leon J. Wood are warmly recommended for background historical material and an overview of Jeremiah's prophetic ministry: *A Survey of Israel's History* (Zondervan) and *The Prophets of Israel* (Baker).
2. William Hendriksen, *Survey of the Bible*, Baker, p. 300.
3. Edward J. Young, *An Introduction to the Old Testament*, Eerdmans, p. 345. The word 'theocracy' indicates God's government of His people.
4. The five *Megilloth* are the five scrolls read by the Jews at the various feasts and fasts: *Canticles,* or the Song of Songs/ Solomon (Passover, commemorating God's deliverance of His people from Egypt); *Ruth* (Pentecost, when the first fruits of the wheat harvest were presented); *Lamentations* (anniversary of the destruction of Jerusalem); *Ecclesiastes* (Tabernacles, which recalled the trials and hardships of God's people when living in booths during the course of their wilderness journey); and *Esther* (Purim, the institution of which is recorded in Esther 9).
5. John Calvin's *Commentary on the Whole Bible,* Baker, volume XI, p. 300.

Chapter 1
1. Here are some scriptures to look up demonstrating this point. For David's conquests and sovereignty over neighbouring states, observe, for example, 2 Samuel 8:1-14 and 10. The extent of Solomon's dominions is revealed in verses like 1 Kings 4:21, 24 and 2 Chronicles 9:22-24. For the power of Judah in the reign of Jehoshaphat see 2 Chronicles 17:10-13 and for Uzziah's reign see 2 Chronicles 26:6-15. Finally, check out Ezra 4:20.

2. Matthew Henry's *Commentary on the Whole Bible,* MacDonald, vol. IV, p. 713.
3. R. K. Harrison, *Jeremiah and Lamentations,* Tyndale Press, p. 207.
4. Lange's *Commentary on the Holy Scriptures,* Jeremiah and Lamentations, Zondervan, p. 41.
5. The hostility of the Edomites against Judah at the destruction of Jerusalem is recorded in Psalm 137:7. The malicious delight of the Ammonites is declared in Ezekiel 25:1-7, and the Moabites, Ammonites and Edomites are all tarred with the same brush in Jeremiah 40:11-16, where special attention is drawn to the behaviour of King Baalis towards Judah.
6. For further profit upon this theme, meditate upon the familiar hymns, 'What a Friend we have in Jesus', 'I've found a Friend, Oh, such a Friend' and 'I have a Friend whose faithful love is more than all the world to me' (numbers 398, 601 and 188 respectively in *Christian Hymns*).
7. Lange's *Commentary,* p. 44.
8. Theo Laetsch, *Bible Commentary,* Jeremiah and Lamentations, Concordia, p. 379.
9. The final word of verse 7 in the NIV is 'destruction', while the AV has 'sabbaths'. It has been observed that this word has given translators and commentators much trouble! 'Destruction, ruin, ruined circumstances' is perhaps best, and enforces the contrast within the verse with her former prosperity. Laetsch translates it 'the cessation of all activity' – literally 'cessations', a play on words on 'sabbath'. He comments that they had refused to keep the divinely appointed day of rest and cessation from labour, and so now a complete cessation of all activity in homes, places of business, courts, the temple, domestic and foreign trade had set in.

    If we were to follow the translation 'sabbaths', then note this: 'The mockery of enemies does not apply to the Jewish celebration of the Sabbath, but to the cessation of the public worship of the Lord, inasmuch as the heathen, by destroying Jerusalem and the temple, fancied they had not only put an end to the worship of the God of the Jews but also conquered the God of Israel as a helpless national deity, and made a mock of Israel's faith in Jahveh [Jehovah] as the only true God' (C.F. Keil and F. Delitzsch, *Commentary on the Old Testament,* Eerdmans, volume VIII, pp. 364-5).

Chapter 2
1. Compare, for example, Joel 4:13; Isaiah 63:2-3; Revelation 14:18-20; 19:15.
2. Keil and Delitzsch, *Commentary,* p. 374.
3. Calvin, *Commentary,* pp. 334-5.

Chapter 3
1. Harrison, *Jeremiah and Lamentations,* p. 214.
2. *The Preacher's Complete Homiletic Commentary,* Baker, vol. 18, p. 43. This excellent work comprises an introduction and exegetical notes by D. G. Watt and expository material by George Barlow.
3. Henry's *Commentary,* p. 721.
4. The word 'dwelling' only occurs here. Some take it as hedge/fence/enclosure; others as hut/tent/thicket. Laetsch observes, 'Whatever its exact meaning, it is certain that the Temple is meant.'
5. Lewes Bayly, *The Practice of Piety* (3rd edition, 1613) – quoted in James T. Dennison Jr. 'The Puritan Doctrine of the Sabbath', *Banner of Truth* magazine, issue 147 (December 1975).
6. Calvin, *Commentary,* p. 355.
7. See Samuel Bolton, *The True Bounds of Christian Freedom,* Banner of Truth Trust.
8. M. Henry, *Commentary,* p. 722.

Chapter 4
1. Ezekiel 13 is another excellent commentary on this.
2. *Preacher's Homiletic Commentary,* p. 42.
3. *Preacher's Homiletic Commentary,* p. 61.

Chapter 5
1. Harrison remarks, 'In many respects this elegy crystallizes the basic themes of Lamentations, and as a foreshadowing of the passion of Jesus Christ has definite affinities with Isaiah 53 and Psalm 22.'
2. *Preacher's Homiletic Commentary,* p. 71.
3. Harrison, *Jeremiah and Lamentations,* p. 224.
4. Benjamin Keach, *Preaching from the Types and Metaphors of the Bible,* Kregel, p. 741.
5. Henry's *Commentary,* p. 727.

Chapter 6
1. Laetsch, *Bible Commentary,* p. 392.
2. *Preacher's Homiletic Commentary,* p. 84.
3. Andrew Bonar, *Diary and Life,* Banner of Truth Trust, p. 355.
4. Henry's *Commentary,* p. 730.

Chapter 7
1. John Flavel, *The Mystery of Providence,* Banner of Truth Trust.
2. A. W. Pink, *The Sovereignty of God,* Banner of Truth Trust, pp. 123ff.
3. See Thomas Watson, *The Doctrine of Repentance,* Banner of Truth Trust.
4. *Preacher's Homiletic Commentary,* p. 97.
5. Laetsch, *Bible Commentary,* p. 393.
6. Henry's *Commentary,* p. 734.

Chapter 8
1. Dr and Mrs Howard Taylor, *Biography of James Hudson Taylor,* Hodder and Stoughton, p. 348.
2. Keil and Delitzsch, *Commentary,* p. 429.
3. Laetsch, *Bible Commentary,* p. 395.

Chapter 9
1. Harrison, *Jeremiah and Lamentations,* pp. 233-4.
2. Cf. Leviticus 26:29; Deuteronomy 28:53-57; 2 Kings 6:24-29.
3. *Preacher's Homiletic Commentary,* p. 108.

Chapter 10
1. Moloch (or Molech) was a god worshipped by the Ammonites. This worship was associated with the sacrifice of children in the fire and was a detestable thing to God (cf. Jeremiah 32:35).
2. Calvin goes on to make an application to Christ and the church, on the basis that if the king is 'the Lord's anointed' and the 'very life breath' of the people, how much more is that true of Christ in His relationship to His church of which He alone is the Head! This is what he says: 'We hence learn that the church is dead, and is like a maimed body, when separated from its Head. If then we desire to live before God, we must come to Christ, who is really the spirit or the breath of our nostrils; for as man that is dead does no longer breathe, so also

we are said to be dead when separated from Christ. On the other hand, as long as there is between Him and us a sacred union, though our life is hid and we die, yet we live in Him, and though we are dead to the world, yet our life is in heaven.'
3.   For example, Jeremiah 49:7-22; Amos 9:12; Obadiah 1-16; Ezekiel 25:12-14; 35:15.
4.   *Preacher's Homiletic Commentary,* p. 119.

Chapter 11
1.   Calvin, *Commentary,* p. 493.
2.   Cf. Proverbs 19:10; 30:21-22; Ecclesiastes 10:7.
3.   Harrison, *Jeremiah and Lamentations,* pp. 239-40.
4.   *Preacher's Homiletic Commentary,* p. 123.

Chapter 12
1.   *Letters of Samuel Rutherford,* Banner of Truth Trust, p. 362.
2.   J. I. Packer, *Knowing God,* Hodder and Stoughton, p. 6.
3.   Because some of the Old Testament prophecies end on what the Jews considered to be a rather negative or gloomy note (e.g. Isaiah 66:24; Malachi 4:6; Lamentations 5:22) it became customary when Old Testament Scripture was read in the synagogue to repeat the penultimate verse so as to end on a more encouraging note. So in the present case verses 21 and 22 would be read in their proper order and then verse 21 would be read a second time. Keil and Delitzsch think (rightly, in my view) that it is not necessary in the case of Lamentations, where, characteristically, complaint and supplication continue to the end, but not without a real element of hope beginning to arise.
4.   Quoted in Lange's *Commentary,* p. 196.

Appendix 1
1.   Thomas Brooks, *Works,* Banner of Truth Trust, vol. 2.

EXODUS
Travelling Homeward
Exodus Simply Explained
Michael Bentley

Michael Bentley provides a clear,
organized exposition of Scripture. His
down-to-earth style helps students of
Scripture, whether preachers or their
congregations, to grasp the meaning of the text without
unnecessary difficulty.

Large paperback, 352 pages, 0 85234 429 5
'...informative, incisive and superb in application...'
John Tindall

1 SAMUEL
Dawn of a Kingdom
The message of 1 Samuel
Gordon J. Keddie

The absolute sovereignty of God and the
triumph of his righteousness are the
principal themes of 1 Samuel. In tracing
the development of Israel from the
anarchy of the period of Judges — from
Samuel the prophet and kingmaker
through Saul, the people's choice, to David, God's chosen
king — the hand of God is seen at work.

Large paperback, 272 pages, 0 85234 248 9
A useful commentary in this fine series.

JOHN'S EPISTLES
Knowing where we Stand
The message of John's epistles
Peter Barnes

In days of spiritual and moral decline we stand in particular need of the message of John's epistles. Right belief, love and obedience are the principal themes explored in this book.

Large paperback, 160 pages, 0 85234 414 7
'...*excellent, thorough, stimulating, informed...*'
John Currid, *Reformed Theological Seminary, Jackson*

JUDE
Slandering the Angels
Jude simply explained
John Benton

Christians may be open to accept anything that causes a sensation and attracts a crowd, even if it departs from the biblical gospel. This commentary helps to combat false teaching and encourages responsible Christian living and practical, loving Christianity for those led astray.

Large paperback, 192 pages, 0 85234 424 4
'...*illuminating exegesis, a fresh and lucid style, a wonderful sprinkling of appropriate and helpful illustrations...*'

Banner of Truth

A wide range of excellent books on spiritual subjects is available from Evangelical Press. Please write to us for your free catalogue or contact us by e-mail.

Evangelical Press
Faverdale North Industrial Estate, Darlington, Co. Durham, DL3 0PH, England

Evangelical Press USA
P. O. Box 84, Auburn, MA 01501, USA

e-mail: sales@evangelical-press.org

web: www.evangelical-press.org